IS YOUR GOD BIG ENOUGH?

MILDRED TENGBOM

First Lutheran Church
of Gray Manor/Library
212 Oakwood Road
Baltimore, Maryland 21222

AUGSBURG PUBLISHING HOUSE
MINNEAPOLIS, MINNESOTA

IS YOUR GOD BIG ENOUGH?

Copyright © 1973 Augsburg Publishing House
Library of Congress Catalog Card No. 72-90261
International Standard Book No. 0-8066-1308-4

All rights reserved. No part of this book may be used or reproduced in any manner whatsoever without written permission except in the case of brief quotations in critical articles and reviews. For information address Augsburg Publishing House, 426 South Fifth Street, Minneapolis, Minnesota 55415.

Scripture quotations unless otherwise noted are from the Revised Standard Version of the Bible, copyright 1946 and 1952 by the Division of Christian Education of the National Council of Churches, and are used by permission.

MANUFACTURED IN THE UNITED STATES OF AMERICA

Contents

PREFACE: Pressures and God 5

Is Your God Big Enough?

When Your Fondest Dreams Crumble 7

When You Are Struck with a Serious Affliction 21

When You Have Enemies 31

When Your Mate Dies 45

When You Can't Get Along with Someone 55

When Your Child Confronts Death 61

When You Feel Trapped in Marriage 71

When You Are Stricken with Cancer 79

When Your Child Dies 91

When You Have to Wait and Wait for an Answer 99

When the Answer Is No 109

When All Human Help Fails 117

AFTERWORD: God Loves and Cares 125

Pressures and God

Water.
We all need it.
So when we were going to build the Bible School complex on the lower slopes of Mount Kilimanjaro in Tanzania, East Africa, one great concern was where would we find adequate water supply for over two hundred people?

Cries of joy and thanksgiving echoed among the hills and valleys the day our African friends found up on the mountainside a spring of clear, bubbling water that flowed so freely we could be assured of a bountiful supply. Pipes were laid to carry the water the three miles down the mountain where it was stored in a huge reservoir. The reservoir sat astride stilts, up high to provide gravity flow to all the buildings on the campus.

One day one of our children asked, "How can water

from the pipe down here on the ground go *up* into the tank?"

"Pressure," we explained. "The constant flow downhill of water in the pipes forces it uphill."

Life is full of pressures. Pressures can help us to "flow upward," to seek God. This little book contains the accounts of people who in various difficult situations turned God-ward and found him big enough to meet their every need.

> *He prayed for health that he might do great things.*
> *He was given infirmity that he might do better things.*
>
> *Poems of Power*

When Your Fondest Dreams Crumble

It seemed incredible. Preaching was Herman Gockel's forte. He had spent eleven years preparing himself for it. Yet here at 32 his dream had dissolved like the mist in the noon sun. For how can you preach without a voice? And his voice was gone. When he tried to preach, that is. His throat would become sore, and his voice vanished. It had been like that for a year now. Palm Sunday, 1938, to be exact, was when he had found himself speechless in the pulpit of Redeemer Lutheran Church in Evansville, Indiana. He consulted 25 different specialists in five different states. They had 25 different things to say. Finally the doctors at the Mayo Clinic had decided it was a psychosomatic condition. It seemed that when Gockel got into the pulpit, he was so anxious to get his message across that his very anxiety constricted his vocal chords so no sound was forthcoming.

The shining diplomas on the wall of his study suddenly seemed to hold little meaning for him. Honors from Concordia College, Fort Wayne, Indiana, in 1926. Honors from Concordia Seminary, St. Louis, in 1931.

He had graduated during the depression slump of the 30s and had been grateful to receive a call to a home mission congregation among sharecroppers. Squishing barefoot through mud as they called on their parishioners had been different from city living for his newly acquired bride, Mildred, and him. For the first few months Sunday attendances fluctuated between twelve and eighteen. But with imagination and creativity, enthusiasm and vigor, the young pastor took hold. He started a radio program of his own, driving sixty miles to the nearest radio station. He sold the local newspaper editor on running a weekly column headed "A Sermon a Week" which appeared in the upper center of the editorial page every week for nearly six years. He began a "direct by mail" approach which carried the gospel to some 200 unchurched families every week. Above all, he rang door bells. And the church grew!

Then, nearly seven years later, came the call to Redeemer Lutheran in Evansville, Indiana. Here the young pastor could preach to hundreds every Sunday! For a period of five months it seemed the magic of the "new broom" was proving itself. The young preacher was in more and more demand. In fact, it was agreed by all that preaching was his strong point. And then suddenly he could preach no more.

He tried, but it was no use. The pain in his throat made continued public speaking out of the question. His preaching voice was gone. So Easter Sunday, 1939, he had the head elder read his farewell, and now they were leaving. He held open the door of their Chevy for his wife, Mildred, and their six-year-old son, Galen, and four-year-old daughter, Greta, who was clasping her live Easter bunny. His recently widowed mother in Cleveland, Ohio, would take them in.

There was nothing melodramatic about his leaving or the days that followed, no hand wringing, no lengthy discussions of their "problems." Excellent Christian training in day school and home had prepared Gockel and his wife to face their problems quietly. But the tragedy had had a numbing effect. They went through the motions of living because life demands we work and eat and sleep. But the zest and joy were gone.

Gockel's wife, Mildred, found a secretarial job. Gockel stayed home and took care of the children. Strange, he thought, as he did the housework, I should be worried about the future. But I'm not. An abiding sense that God was in control, that he was preparing him, that he had a plan he was working out, never left Gockel. During those days a verse frequently emerged from his subconscious. He had learned it in Christian day school, at college, and at the seminary. Now it really meant something to him. "He who did not spare his own Son, but gave him up for us all, will he not also give us all things with him?" (Romans 8:32). With Job he found himself confessing: "I had heard of thee by the hearing of the ear, but now my eye sees thee" (Job 42:5). He began to see and understand the ways and words of God more clearly.

The first door of opportunity swung open six months later. It was to answer mail that came in response to Dr.

Walter Maier's Lutheran Hour. He went to St. Louis on probation, and remained "on probation" until retirement 32 years later. Life always was to hold a tentative quality for him. He never knew what was ahead. Like Abraham of old God was to call him again and again to go to "a land he knew not."

He was grateful for sporadic opportunities for additional work. He wrote innumerable rhymed verses for Christmas cards at 25c a line. During peak seasons, especially before Christmas, he pushed a truck in the shipping department of Concordia from 5 P.M. to 10 P.M. filling orders for Christmas merchandise. He embraced "time and a half" as a gift from heaven.

All the while, quietly and unseen to others, God was at work in Gockel's heart. Gradually he realized that he amounted to nothing—except the Lord bless him. God was the potter. He was only clay. God held his future in his hands. God was going to run things. Little by little humility and pliability, wisdom, judgment, tact, patience and evenness of temper began to manifest themselves in his life. He was going to need this fruit of the Spirit in the years ahead for exacting commissions.

Other appointments followed: Assistant Executive Secretary of the Lutheran Laymen's League, Advertising Manager of Concordia Publishing House, Assistant Executive Secretary of the Board for Missions in North and South America, Editor of *Today*. He helped launch and served on the editorial boards of *The St. Louis Lutheran, This Day,* and *The American Lutheran* (forerunner of *The Lutheran Forum*).

A pattern was beginning to emerge. Just as he began to feel comfortable in a new work, he would be called to another. The fine creative mind God had given him was being used. In almost every case he was called to begin a new work, to envision the possibilities, to develop it. And then he had to move on. Always too, the assignment seemed to call for more than the man thought he possessed. God was teaching his servant to listen for his call, to believe God would enable him, and then to step out in faith and obedience.

Meanwhile God was testing and preparing his servant through suffering. His wife repeatedly was ill, in 1945 critically ill. Spiritual stress and pain introduced Gockel to a more intimate relationship with God. Out of that came a book, *What Jesus Means to Me,* that has become a classic with sales of over 300,000. It has been put in Braille, cut on records for the blind, and translated into Spanish, Japanese, Russian, and Hindi.

The little book is vibrant with the testimony of what Jesus had come to mean to Herman Gockel. Listen to the declarations:

"Of all things that Jesus means to me He is, above all else, my Savior."

"I have felt the dreadful weight of sin. Again and again I have had to say with the Apostle Paul: 'I know that in me (that is, in my flesh) dwelleth no good thing.' "

"Jesus means to me . . . forgiveness!"

"I am at peace with God. I am at peace with myself . . . I am at peace in the midst of conflict . . . I am at peace beneath the weight of every burden."

"I have found in Jesus Christ, my great Provider, who cares for all my needs, both temporal and spiritual. . . . Can I be sure that each succeeding day will

11

find a sufficient measure of His grace and goodness to see me and my loved ones through? Yes, I can be sure."

"Scarcely an hour passes without my being clearly conscious of his presence. Again and again I find myself in earnest conversation, sharing with him my problems and perplexities, seeking guidance and direction."

"It would be foolish and untrue to say that the Christian life does not have its trials. The gnawing pang of loneliness, the heavy hand of sickness, the bitter pain of disappointment, the icy finger of inevitable death—all of these fall to the lot of the Christian as they do to every man. But there is a difference, a great difference! Through Christ the believer knows he is at peace with God; and being at peace with his Maker, he knows that even sorrow and sickness and death are part of God's gracious plan for him."

"Inasmuch as I am a child of God through faith in Jesus Christ, the future holds more good for me than I could ever hope for. Christ is my Guarantee of a blessed future."

"From Christ I have learned the meaning and purpose of life. I am no longer baffled by its evils, its disappointments and its heartaches."

"I have found that, no matter what the circumstances, no matter how fraught with gloom the prospect, no matter how discouraging or disconcerting the difficulty—I could nevertheless tap that reservoir of joy which God has placed into every human heart that has come to Him through Christ."

"What comfort, what strength, what joy are mine— in the knowledge that beyond the portals of eternity there lies a friendly Father's house!"

The testing was to continue over the years. Twenty-six times Mildred Gockel moved in and out of hospitals. Six times she walked up to death's door but turned back. As the testings continued more books poured from Dr. Gockel's pen: *My Father's World, Answer to Anxiety, The Cross and the Common Man, My Hand in His, Give Your Life a Lift* and dozens of pamphlets and devotional booklets and hundreds of newspaper articles.

Sorrow and pain, brought to the cross, set the heart singing. Dr. Gockel let his heart sing through a number of Christian hymns he composed for children. Best known is "Jesus Loves Children," sung to the melody of "Rock-a-bye, Baby," and published in many hymn books for children.

Then in 1951 the biggest appointment of all came.

In 1950 and 1951 two significant developments had occurred. In 1951, through their "Conquest for Christ" offering, the Lutheran Church, Missouri Synod gathered in $14,500,000 for missionary expansion. The writer of the promotional materials had been Dr. Gockel.

The previous year a small committee met in Medart's restaurant near Concordia Seminary in St. Louis. Included on that committee were such well-known names in Christian broadcasting as Dr. Eugene R. Bertermann, Rev. Herman W. Gockel, Rev. Oswald C. J. Hoffmann, and Prof. Leonard C. Wuerffel. The meeting was but the first of many.

As a result of the recommendation of that committee, the following year, 1951, the Board of Directors of the Missouri Synod voted an allocation of $750,000 from the "Conquest for Christ" offering for the first year of the Synod's television ministry. Rev. Gockel was called as Religious Director of the program. Gockel really did not want the job. He wanted to stay with the magazine *Today*. He enjoyed that work immensely.

"I was hesitant to accept the position as religious director of the TV program," Dr. Gockel says. "So much was involved. Our purpose in every episode was to bring out two basic doctrines of Scripture: man's sin and God's grace in Christ. We could not be satisfied with just a moral story. But most of our viewers, we knew, live their lives almost exclusively on a horizontal plane (man to man). Seldom are they conscious of the vertical dimension (man to God). I knew it would require a great deal of skill to direct our viewer's thoughts God-ward without it seeming unnatural or preachy. And we had to do it all in 27 minutes and 52 seconds—developing characters, building an exciting plot, and weaving in a verbalization of the gospel message that would not seem forced.

"I knew too that taking the position would mean dividing my time between St. Louis and Hollywood. I would have to be a catalyst between the script committee in St. Louis and the producers in Hollywood. I knew this would mean being away from home much of the time. Also film production has so many unpredictables and uncontrollables. You are dependent on so many people: the script writer, the actors and actresses, the director, the film editor. The work would be emotionally, mentally, and physically demanding. But I sensed God, through his church, was leading me into it, so I went ahead."

Although TV was new in America in 1951, sales of sets had soared to 12 million. More than 100 commercial broadcasting stations announced they were in business.

Family Films of Hollywood was employed as the production company. Endless script meetings were held. Principles and guidelines were defined. During November and December, 1951, the first two pilot films were produced and in January, 1952, they were premiered at the Missouri Synod's Fiscal Conference held in St. Louis. By the fall of 1952, twenty-six episodes of "This Is the Life" were ready to be aired. September, 1952, the first episode went out over a few stations. The response was immediate. *Newsweek, Christian Century, Saturday Evening Post,* and *Life* all commented favorably.

For the next twenty years the warehouse-like room at Family Films, Hollywood, became Dr. Gockel's pulpit. The setting was quite different from a cathedral. In the studio sturdy crude wooden platforms overhead support huge lamps to provide overhead lighting and supplementary lights for highlighting and shadow effects. Wooden boardwalks connect one platform with another. A maze of heavy black cords snake their way overhead from one end of the building to the other.

On street level a variety of room sets crouch like rabbit hutches: living rooms—fancy and dilapidated—dining rooms, kitchens, and an outdoor scene. Props not in use stand against the walls. A mobile camera is mounted on a moveable platform. There are no windows. Walls and ceilings are soundproofed. The only connection with the outside world is the voice of a switchboard girl over the P.A. calling someone to the phone, or the occasional droning of a plane overhead.

Seated in a battered director's chair with his name printed across the back, Dr. Gockel directed his 25-member crew: microphone boom man, production manager, prop man, sound mixers, grips, makeup artists, camera man, and director. They worked as one man. When "frustration vibrations" rippled across to Gockel, he would simply raise his cane. "I learned to know the men so well that I could tell from the back of their necks when their blood pressure went up," Gockel recalls smiling. "That's why I carried a cane. It was really the only cane I could raise."

Dr. Gockel's dedication to the message of the series soon got through to the crew members. Affectionately they dubbed him, "Sin-and-Grace Gockel."

Dr. Gockel soon discovered that he was responsible for many things he hadn't thought about. "Like checking necklines," he shared. "It would have been bad for me in St. Louis if I had slipped on that." He chuckled. "Hemlines were also my responsibility. Believe it or not, once I asked the wardrobe mistress to *shorten* an actress's dress by four inches."

As Dr. Gockel had guessed, being director of the program did involve running for taxis and planes and living as a displaced person a third of each year. By the end of 20 years he estimated over 2,000 nights had been spent in hotels, and over 6,000 meals eaten in restaurants.

But the response to the program made it all infinitely worthwhile and rewarding. More and more doors opened. Today approximately 500 stations carry the program weekly. The roster of countries outside the United States which flash the weekly drama on their television screens reads like the table of contents in a geography book: Antigua, Australia, Bermuda, Canada, Costa Rica, Ecuador, Ethiopia, Ghana, Guatemala, Jamaica, Liberia, Mauritius, Mexico, Netherlands, Netherlands Antilles,

Nigeria, Philippines, Rhodesia, Sierra Leone, Surinam, Trinidad, Upper Volta, and Zambia. It is broadcast in English, Spanish, and French. It is also carried on the Armed Forces Radio and TV series. Our family had viewed it in Nairobi, Kenya, East Africa, some years ago.

It is estimated that over five million view the program weekly. The program has received 25 different awards, both for technical excellence and for its contribution to the spiritual life of the nation.

The most significant indication of the effectiveness of the program, however, lies in the 2,000 letters from viewers that pour in weekly. Most write requesting booklets which are offered. Several million booklets have been distributed, all Christ-centered, Bible-based, and spelling out the way of salvation.

About sixty letters come weekly in response to the invitation given at the close of each program: "If you have a spiritual problem and no one to advise you, *This Is the Life* will be happy to give you the counsel of God's Word." These letters Dr. Gockel answered personally on the lonely Saturdays and Sundays he spent in his hotel room in Hollywood. He relied heavily on tracts, pamphlets, and booklets which zero in on the particular problem of the troubled one. A favorite booklet was the 60-page booklet he wrote back in 1954, *God's Invitation to You*. He also referred the writer to a nearby church, giving the name, address, telephone number of church and pastor, and the hours of worship service, if possible.

Some letters told dramatic stories of lives changed.

"The most rewarding aspect of my work," Dr. Gockel declares, "was the realization that the Lord, having seen fit to silence my voice in the parish pulpit, placed before me a microphone, amplifying my voice so it could be heard by millions. It really wasn't my choice. The Lord led. I followed."

Which explains why the preacher who was "scared speechless" was able later to preach to millions.

Dr. Gockel retired in 1971. "The past two years I had had a bout with heart failure and one with triple staph pneumonia," he explained. "Each laid me aside for five weeks. I recognized the Lord's amber light for me. I thought it was only exercising better stewardship of my primary talent, writing, that I retire."

So the pen is busy again, telling the story of God's matchless grace in Christ Jesus. Wife, Mildred, who has survived her myriad illnesses, is fit and well. She does her own housework and yard work and two days a week serves as Gray Lady at a Lutheran Hospital.

The lives of Dr. and Mrs. Gockel bear quiet and noble witness to what happens when men seek God's will for their lives and walk with him. Life then surpasses their fondest dreams.

What to Do When Our Fondest Dreams Crumble

The Christian needs to understand that the way of the world is different from the way of Jesus. The world says: Be ambitious. Chart your own course. Strive to succeed. Rely on yourself. It's all up to you. Toot your own horn. See that you get to the top.

The way of Jesus declares: the single most important thing is that you are rightly related to God through Christ. This right relationship is made evident by a commitment to Christ, a desire and willingness to seek, understand, and follow his plan.

Sometimes his plan is at variance with ours. Often it seems to include tasks that seem beyond us. This is to keep us relying, not on our own resources, but on his. And usually, following him will involve a cross, points where our will will be crossed by God's will, and we have to choose to go God's way. This involves suffering, but the fact is that God prepares his people through suffering, pain, disappointments, set-backs. Only thus can character be produced. Only thus do we learn to know God. Strangely enough, though, this way of the cross and of suffering leads to deep, satisfying joy.

When we yield ourselves to God and begin to ask, "Father, what do you want me to do?" a whole new life of adventure begins. Through prayer we explore avenues of service that might be open to us. Beneath our groping, questioning fingers, as we move down walls, here and there we shall find the walls giving way and we discover doors. Then by faith we must step through those open doors and launch out into the unknown, trusting God to give us all we need. Again and again we will be astonished at the way God answers prayer and works for those who wait for him. Life will become joyous and purposeful and rewarding. There is no joy the world can offer which can compare with the joy of living in companionship with God and being his co-worker. Only then do we begin to realize our potential. The way of Jesus is open to us all.

> *Our best method of awaiting the great exchange of worlds is to go on doing the duties of life.*
> —F. B. MEYER

When You Are Struck with a Serious Affliction

It was 10 P.M. October 20, 1970. Thirty-nine-year-old Rev. Robert Lange, pastor of Mount of Olives Lutheran Church, Mission Viejo, California, but now a patient at South Coast Hospital in Laguna Beach, had been waiting all day for the neurologist to come to his bedside. Several weeks earlier when he had first noticed weakness and stiffness in his legs, he had attributed it to arthritis. But increasing weakness alarmed him. He went to his doctor. Five days of intensive testing in the hospital followed. Bob Lange wondered now what the results of the tests would be.

The door to his room was pushed noiselessly open. The neurologist stepped inside. Preliminary greetings. Then, "The tests show that you have amyotrophic lateral sclorosis."

"And what is that?"

"It's a degenerative disease which involves massive muscle deterioration. Perhaps it is better known as creeping paralysis."

"Is it curable?"

"No."

The doctor pulled up a chair and sat down. Lange saw tears in his eyes.

"The prognosis?"

"About 3 years—80% of the cases die within 3 years' time. The remaining 20% live on for 15, 20 years."

Lange was silent.

"Hopefully there will be a breakthrough for a cure in 10 years. Now there is basically nothing we can do."

"He didn't say it in just those words," Lange recalls now, "but the message I got was that I should go home and prepare to die. The nurse came with a sedative, but I didn't sleep that night. Death is the most traumatic event in a person's life. You know how it is—it's always going to be George, not you. When it *is* you, it is a profound shock in every way: physically, emotionally, mentally."

A friend came by the hospital the next day and brought Lange home. Alone at home he waited for his wife, Magdalene, to come home from teaching elementary school at El Toro Base. He debated whether or not to tell her. I won't, he thought, then—but it's just postponing it. She'll wonder and worry at the progressive weakness.

"So I told her," Lange says. "We both wept together for about an hour. That was psychologically good though. The children came home, sensed something serious was wrong and tiptoed out, giving us the solitude we needed at that hour."

Bob and Magdalene Lange set about at once to put things in order. They drew up a will. Their extended family is not large. Bob has two sisters. Magdalene is an only child. They made provision for their children in the event that both of them should die. They decided it would be easier for Magdalene and the children to stay on in familiar surroundings. They were living in a parsonage. The church council arranged for them to purchase the parsonage. Magdalene already had her lifetime certification for teaching, so that was taken care of.

"We wanted the crisis to be a learning experience for our children—Catherine, 10, and Mark, 12," Lange explained. "We didn't want to load them with too heavy responsibilities. At the same time they would have to learn to accept a difficult situation and trust. They have questions, of course. Mark wants to know why we can send men to the moon and not find a cure for my legs. Every time there is more deterioration the children look worried. 'Maybe you're just tired today,' they say hopefully. But when the deterioration persists, they have to accept. Lou Gehrig's story of how he was stricken with the disease was shown on TV. The children watched it on two successive nights. It helped explain things I had had trouble explaining to them, like how death comes when the paralysis hits a vital organ. It was helpful for Mark, who is a baseball player himself, to see that even a robust, healthy player like Gehrig was struck.

"If only," handsome, composed Bob Lange leans back in his swivel chair, forehead accordion-wrinkled now, "if only I can help them see that it is better to master our crisis instead of letting our crisis master us . . . if only I can leave them with the assurance that God loves them—

he isn't an old meanie—and their father loved them . . . then I shall be happy."

During the following months in his congregational planning, more than ever, Pastor Lange bore in mind that someone would succeed him. What could he do so it would be easy for his successor either to build on what he already had laid or introduce changes—whichever he thought better. How could he cultivate a teachable, adaptable attitude among his people?

He decided also to share openly with his parishioners the conflicts he personally experienced. Would it not enrich them? Could he not only demonstrate how to die, but also leave them with the unshakable faith that life does not end when the casket is closed?

He thought of the community in which they lived. Their church, Mount of Olives, was unique in that it was a planned feature of a planned city, Mission Viejo. The church buildings arose before there were enough residences to supply families to fill the church. Mission Viejo, population 13,000, lies between Los Angeles and San Diego. Developed on 11,000 acres, it was centered around a million-dollar golf course and a $300,000 recreation center. Houses are priced from $23,000 (stripped, no carpeting or landscaping) to $67,000. Incomes run from $10,000 to $30,000 a year. The town itself, at the outset was a walled community. Alarmed at the changes they saw taking place in society, educated, highly successful, affluent young people sought to withdraw. They wanted to escape from drugs, riots, race problems, smog. They felt little or no responsibility toward these problems.

But they soon discovered that the problems they were

trying to flee were right in their midst. The past years have marked a change in attitude. There is more openness and willingness now to accept responsibility. Well-groomed Bob Lange, who dresses with good taste and carries himself with poise and ease, had fit well into the community. He combines compassion with dignity, reserve with friendliness. Quietly, kindly, he calls to people to be master of things, not to let things master them. Now because of his serious affliction the community again was being given an opportunity to reevaluate life's concerns.

During occasional quiet times, Bob Lange has thought deeply about the legacy he wants to leave. Material things suddenly seemed of little consequence. With his wife, his children, the people of his church, the community, and his friends he hopes to leave something of himself. He hopes that love will help them pass it on and thus stepping stones will be laid for a better world. He hopes to leave goals others can attempt to reach, to demonstrate what it means to be a man, a husband, and a father. His primary relationship to his family has become more meaningful than ever.

"Some may think," he observed, "that just because a man's work or calling absorbs most of his time, therefore it is most important to him. But that is not true. Whether or not a man succeeds in his family relationships is of primary importance to him."

Days of darkness and depression come too. Acceptance is always difficult. To regress from walker to wheelchair was an adjustment with which he still has not made peace.

When the dark days come, he turns to God. "God has

provided a way for us through Christ," he says. "When one is rightly related to God, help just does come. Power. Strength. Hope. They just are there. All one needs to do is to be open to receive help. Let it flow in. Don't push or strive. Simply say, 'Lord, I'm in a mess. I need you like I've never needed you before. Help me.' And help does come."

Lange has discovered that the crisis has brought a new openness before God for him, a new awareness that God loves him. He is grateful he is being given time to prepare. On his best days he finds himself even looking forward with joy and anticipation. "Life doesn't end," he says eagerly. "It is just intensified with God."

Always, of course, he clings to tiny glimmers of hope. Consultation with the Mayo Clinic directed him to Houston. He became one of a second group of 30 receiving a new drug. At its best, so far, the drug seems only to be slowing down the progress of the disease.

Letters from all over the country have come urging him to seek miraculous healing. Lange holds himself in readiness, asking himself if he has prepared himself sufficiently so he could be equally receptive to healing or no results.

The ties of earth are strong. He is concerned about Magdalene, about the children. He wishes he could be with them as they go through high school. When these anxieties mount, he turns to prayer. He begins by thanking God that he is alive, that there seem to be small indications of improvement in some ways, that he is able to work.

Work is a wonderful therapy. Magdalene tackles a stack

of papers needing to be corrected. Pastor Lange loses himself in the work of the parish, so completely, in fact, that the majority of the time he is not even thinking of his affliction.

Friends support. "How much it means," Lange states, "when without apology a friend comes and says, 'I'd like to fix the shutters on your house as my gift to you, because I love you.' This reassurance that people care helps so much, because the one caught in a crisis situation feels very alone."

Children help more than they realize. Lange's home, built on a hillside, is tri-level. It became necessary to install a chair lift so Lange could get to the different levels. He found himself regarding the lift a bit resentfully until he noted the evident delight of the children over their new "toy." Then acceptance became easier.

The examples of others cheer and encourage. Books have been a great help, especially *Through the Valley of the River Kwai* by Ernest Gordon, *I'm OK—You're OK* by Thomas Harris, *Habitation of Dragons* by Keith Miller and *Time for God* and *Salute to the Sufferer* by Leslie Weatherhead.

"And then," Bob Lange's face lights up with his warm, contagious smile, "there's music. My parents gave us a piano. The first song we sang, as we gathered around it was 'Now Thank We All Our God.' When doubts nag and peace is threatened, we go to the piano and play and sing—a little loudly perhaps—but it sure helps chase the gloom away. God is with us. He is helping us grow in our faith that he will see us through, that he will not forsake us."

What to Do When You Are Struck with a Serious Affliction:

Be realistic about it. An African legend tells the story of a mother hen who tried to teach her baby chicks to be on the alert for the chicken hawk. "When his shadow falls on the ground, run and get under my wings," she said. But one little chick thought he was wiser than his mother. The next time when the dreaded hawk's shadow fell on the ground, this little chick simply tucked his head under his own wing. "That way," he reasoned, "I won't see the hawk." The last that was heard of the little chick was his squawking in terror as the chicken hawk bore him away in his claws. So don't try to deceive yourself. Face the truth.

Don't hit yourself over your head if you discover you are angry, disappointed, frustrated, or depressed. This is natural. God understands. Be patient. This will pass. As you hang on and seek God's help he will enable you to accept your affliction.

Put things in order. If you are married, discuss with your mate insurance policies and provisions, bank accounts, and payments that have to be made monthly. If your disease is of the nature that it quite likely will be terminal soon, you may even want to express your wishes in regard to final arrangements. This can be done without being morbid. Settling these matters can bring relief and a measure of peace. Above all else, if something is troubling you spiritually, seek help. God doesn't want us to live under a burden of guilt or uncertainty or be chewed by fear or anxiety. If our hearts are at rest in God, we can bear an amazing amount of stress.

Be thankful and grateful for everything you can. Praise. Sing. Remember that praise can be a matter of the will. "I will bless the Lord at all times," the psalmist declared. "Will" indicates resolute, determined decision. Agreeable emotions may or may not accompany this decision. The important thing is the inclination of the heart.

Be frank in telling God how you feel. It won't affect his attitude toward you. He loves you. If you can't put your thoughts and emotions into words, turn to God mutely. Just turning to him is faith.

Don't be too proud to accept help from others.

Keep as busy and involved with others as you can.

Continue to hope. Explore new avenues of healing that may be open to you.

Don't isolate yourself. The testimonies of others who have been through similar experiences can help. Books help also.

Take a day at a time. When a bad day comes get through it by saying hopefully, "Maybe tomorrow will be better." It often is.

Select a few Bible verses that positively affirm God's love for you and his promise to help. Write these on cards. Read them every morning and evening. Better yet, memorize them. They will slip into your subconscious and become a well of strength and courage for you. A few verses you might find helpful are: Isaiah 41:10; Isaiah 41:13; I Peter 5:7; Philippians 4:6, 7; Philippians 4:19; Isaiah 26:3; Psalm 34:4-6.

> Love your enemies, do good to those who hate you, bless those who curse you, pray for those who abuse you.
>
> —JESUS

When You Have Enemies

He was loved by his enemies, hated and scorned by his countrymen, cherished as a foster father by children of a different race than his. Passionately devoted to his country involved in war, he fervently desired peace.

After his story had been telecast from London, reserved Britishers who recognized him in the subways and on the streets stopped to tell him that they had been moved to tears.

He is Kiyoshi Watanabe, Lutheran pastor in southern Japan. Here is his story.

The wheels of the train gradually gained momentum, bearing Watanabe farther and farther down the track. He leaned out the window and caught one last glimpse of Mitsuko, leaning against a lamp post crying. He slumped to his seat. Houses and trees blurred. He lost himself in reverie.

His thoughts wandered back to the day his older brother, Hidezi, brought him the Bible which changed his life. He was ordained into the ministry when he was only 25.

He married and his wife, Shigaru, bore him two daughters and one son. For seven years life flowed along serenely and happily. Then in two days' time the little daughters were stricken with a disease and died. The birth of another daughter, Miwa, brought comfort. And then Shigaru became pregnant again.

In the coach now Watanabe shifted his position and pressed his head against the coolness of the glass. He closed his eyes and Shigaru's face was before him again— wan, tired, but happy. She placed in his arms a beautiful boy, his son. And then she died.

Shigaru's face faded, and Watanabe saw again Mitsuko, his second wife, back on the railroad platform. The gentle, responsive, tiny kindergarten teacher who had come into his life had embraced not only him but his three small children too. It disturbed Watanabe that Mitsuko was so broken about his leaving now. She had not wept even when he left for two years to study theology in the United States.

So many things changed during those two years he was gone. Signs of military preparedness were everywhere evident when he returned. It created a conflict in his heart between pride in his great country and horror at the thought of becoming involved in a war.

Other changes had taken place too. His church in Hiroshima had been closed. Both Watanabe and Mitsuko had to turn to teaching. The draft claimed their two sons. And then Watanabe himself received a letter from the war department. Because he was fluent in English, they wanted him to serve as civilian interpreter to the army.

It was this appointment that was carrying Watanabe farther and farther away from Mitsuko and his children now. Suddenly the pain of all the separations Watanabe had suffered in his life were too much for him. On the railroad coach he covered his face with his hands and sobbed.

His assignment, he discovered, was to the Prison Camps at Hong Kong where he was to work under Colonel Tokunaga. British soldiers, sailors, and airmen were interned at the camp. Watanabe had expected to experience a feeling of triumph the first time he saw the vanquished enemies of his country. He hadn't realized being a Christian would make a difference. When he actually saw the prisoners, emaciated, thin, ragged, and dirty, he was dismayed. To Inouye, another interpreter, he protested, "To despise, to mistreat, to hate like this is not the way of God!"

Inouye's face froze. "God? So you are a Christian?"

Inouye quickly circulated the word that Interpreter Watanabe was a weak man, a possible traitor to his country, a man to be watched. Watanabe knew he was a marked man. But he also knew he had to respond like a Christian.

Watanabe's first witnessing of the interrogation of a British soldier was something he could never forget. The slapping, the punching of the helpless prisoner made Watanabe shrink. And when he saw the heavy belt buckle bite into the naked chest of the Britisher and heard him groan with pain, it was too much for Watanabe. He ran from the room and sought refuge in the lavatory. There he was sick. Then he sobbed, with handkerchief crammed in his mouth.

33

In his despair he dropped to his knees. He prayed for forgiveness for himself, for Inouye, for his nation. He sought help and strength. It was given. Peace filled his heart. He arose from his knees.

"I am a coward," he admitted to himself. "I am afraid of pain. I am afraid of the future and what might happen to me. But I have to be loyal to God. God, you will have to help me."

After that day Watanabe walked straighter and more briskly. As he was able, in small ways, he showed kindnesses and courtesy to the prisoners. The assurance he was doing right was his reward.

One day when he was alone in the camp office a petite young British woman, mother of three, came in. Both her husband and father were prisoners in the camp. Could she see them? she asked. As she talked Watanabe wondered if she could be the outside contact person he needed to get supplies he needed for the prisoners. Hesitantly he asked her. She was willing to help.

So began the friendship between Nellie Lee and her three children and Kiyoshi Watanabe. Watanabe became confidant, comforter and supporter to Nellie Lee. Her children, in turn, promptly adopted Watanabe, called him "Uncle John." On Sundays when he visited them they entwined their arms around his neck and shared joys and troubles. During those happy hours Watanabe was able to forget some of the horrors of his week-day prison world.

Nellie Lee introduced Watanabe to Dr. Selwyn-Clarke, former director of Medical and Sanitary Services, Hong Kong, who was now in hiding. He provided Watanabe with medicines and medical equipment to smuggle to the British doctors imprisoned in the camp. It was a dangerous thing to do. Watanabe knew if he was caught he could be killed.

Could he ever forget the first time? As he neared the gates, carrying his small leather bag, it seemed to him that all the Japanese soldiers standing around outside the camp were looking at him. But at the gate the sentries were only mildly curious. They let him pass and Watanabe tried to walk casually towards his hut. Were the sentries staring after him, he wondered. Following him? With great difficulty he continued walking, praying that his trembling legs would hold him up. At last, his hut. He pushed the case under the bed and collapsed on a chair.

Now how was he to deliver it? What was the name of the British doctor who was to receive it? His mind went blank. He panicked. Then he remembered thoughtful Nellie putting a note in his pocket. Ah, there was the name! Dr. Ashton-Rose.

Watanabe waited until it was dark, then set off with the case. Trembling again and sweating, he chided himself for being a coward.

Stepping inside Ashton-Rose's hut quickly he pushed the case toward him. "From Dr. Selwyn-Clarke. Please, I need a receipt."

Ashton-Rose was uncommunicative.

Outside in the dark a sentry was approaching. In agony Watanabe pleaded, "Please hurry."

The doctor opened the case. He stared in disbelief and amazement. Then hurriedly he scrawled his name on a piece of paper. Watanabe slipped outside. He rounded the edge of the building just as the sentry was passing out of sight. The sentry must have heard something, for he stopped. Watanabe stood rigid, biting on his thumb in an effort to keep his chattering teeth quiet. Finally the sentry moved on.

In his room Watanabe reached his bed just before he fainted. He regained consciousness to find himself vomiting on the floor.

Watanabe had hoped, as he continued to carry in the articles of mercy, that he would be able to overcome his fear and walk calmly and nonchalantly. But with each successive trip his fear increased. Finally he resigned himself to even this. So what if he was a coward? Even cowards could obey God if they willed to do so. And he did.

But ultimately Watanabe's missions of mercy came under suspicion, and the officials transferred him to the hospital on Bowen Road. In one way Watanabe welcomed the transfer. Being in cleaner surroundings and away from physical punishment and shootings might help, he thought. Maybe God understood that he had almost reached the saturation point in witnessing senseless suffering. Nightmares were tormenting him, and when he would awaken, perspiring, he would begin to think of Mitsuko and the children. Sometimes in his loneliness he would cry. Maybe, he thought, working in the hospital will be better.

Back in Hiroshima Mitsuko Watanabe tried to cope with the problems of her kindergarten students. She worried about her own children too, scattered now. She worried about her husband too, lest army life be too hard on his gentle, sympathetic, and sensitive nature.

She worried about the outcome of the war too. The older children, Miwa and Heidizi, thought the Americans would be attacking Japan soon, that Hiroshima was endangered. They begged their mother and sister to leave. Mitsuko wondered if she could find work if she went to another city. And how could she leave the kindergarten children who were so dependent on her? She wrote to her husband. What should she do? she asked.

When Watanabe received her letter he was puzzled how to answer. The reason Mitsuko had given him for wanting to leave Hiroshima had been cut from her letter. "Do as you think best," was all he could advise. "God will guide you."

Then Watanabe learned that the Japanese had captured Dr. Selwyn-Clarke. The news plunged him into deepest despair. Sleepless nights started to plague him again.

At the hospital boredom hung heavy over the beds. Watanabe tried to discover what the interests of the patients were, and then he tried to provide them with paints, pens, paper, books. And always he tried to keep hope alive.

Food supplies began to run short. When Nellie Lee's family felt the pinch Uncle John shared with them some of his monthly check and tried to salvage food from the kitchen to bring to them.

Reports began to leak through that the Japanese forces were no longer making advances in the Pacific. Dr. Saito, the hospital administrator, considered the defeats his country was suffering as personal insults. He wore a revolver as he walked around the hospital. He screamed and ranted and issued irrational orders.

The day the first American plane flew over Hong Kong he went completely berserk. The men, lying in their beds, heard the plane first and listened with unbelieving ears. Then the ward filled with a resounding cheer. Dr. Saito tore into the ward.

"Who cheered?" he screamed as he ran from bed to bed. The hospital became deathly still. Dr. Saito ordered the men out of bed and on parade. Then he walked down the line, striking out viciously at the men. Watanabe was deeply ashamed and embarrassed that one of his countrymen had degraded himself in such a way. That night, in a letter to Mitsuko, he wrote everything he had ever thought about Dr. Saito. Then he tore it up and carefully burned it. But he felt better.

For some reason, the blame for the entire incident was placed on Watanabe and he was transferred to Stanley Camp. It was at Stanley Camp one day that a tall and unbelievably thin prisoner was led in. His hair was snow white, his face furrowed with lines of deep pain and suffering. Watanabe stared, then ran across the office floor. "Dr. Selwyn-Clarke, what have they done to you?"

The doctor's arm went around Watanabe's shoulder. Gentle words of comfort were poured into his ear. And then the doctor was led away. It was only then that Watanabe realized that Colonel Tokunaga was in the room and had witnessed the entire incident.

"Traitor!" the Colonel snarled. "Now you are going to die! You're going to bleed and scream and suffer. How are you going to like that?"

Watanabe was silent.

"You are going to leave Stanley Camp. You may go anywhere you wish. The Kempeitai will be watching you. When they want to, they will take you."

The next weeks are fuzzy in Watanabe's memory. He doesn't know where he went. Or what he did. Or how he ate and kept alive. He remembers only one brief period of consciousness. He woke to find it was stifling hot. He was sweating profusely. There were a couple of mosquitoes inside his net, and he tried to find them. He fell asleep again only to be enmeshed in a nightmare in which Mitsuko and he were struggling to overcome some strange, unknown Thing that threatened to overpower and choke them.

Back in Hiroshima, Miwa, eldest surviving daughter, stood at the door of her mother's home. "I've come for you, Mother. Tomorrow morning early we must leave. I have arranged transportation."

"God be praised!" Mitsuko could utter no more.

At 7:17 A.M. the next day, Monday, August 6, 1945, the atom bomb was dropped over the city of Hiroshima.

Compassionate people found Watanabe wandering aimlessly in the streets and took him in. Slowly memory returned to him. What had happened to Mitsuko in Hiroshima he wondered. And then the news came over the radio. It wasn't the whole story nor the true story, but what Watanabe heard was too much. Suddenly he felt very old and very cold inside.

Together with the other Japanese Watanabe was interned. Dr. Selwyn-Clarke appealed for him and he was given a position as interpreter at Kowloon Hospital. Though he was treated well, still, little by little, he failed. Mrs. Doughty, one of the English ladies whom he had helped at Stanley Camp, noted it with concern. Gently she probed for the reason. One day it poured out: "I can't bear any longer not hearing from Hiroshima and not knowing what has happened to Mitsuko. Is there no way to find out?"

The first gleam of real hope came when a naval officer visited the Doughtys. He was going to Kure. "I'll try to get news for you," the naval man promised. "But don't hope for too much."

A few weeks later Mrs. Doughty handed Watanabe a letter. "Perhaps you would like to be alone while you read this," she suggested.

He went to the room that was his when he visited the Doughtys. He sat down on the bed, turning the letter around in his hands, praying for courage to open it. At last he took a deep breath and tore open the envelope. The handwriting was his daughter's, Kimi's.

He read it right through to the end. Then he cried as he had never cried before.

Miwa had gone to escort her mother, Mitsuko, out of Hiroshima, Kimi wrote. They had planned to leave early, but it was not early enough. Kimi herself had gone to Hiroshima to search for them. The only thing she could identify was the fitting of her mother's handbag. Mitsuko and Miwa had just disintegrated.

Watanabe laid down on the bed and turned his face to the wall. His heart ached. For two days and two nights he lay with his grief. At last, little by little, he was able to accept what had happened. He was able to forgive those men who had dropped the bomb. He couldn't understand why it had happened, but, as always, he was ready to trust God.

Many years ago he had given himself to God. He had told the Lord at that time he would try to do God's will. He had tried. He would continue to try. And for all that happened to him while he pursued the course he, Kiyoshi Watanabe, could trust God.

What to Do When You Have Enemies

Differentiate between "inherited" enemies and personal enemies. "Inherited" enemies are those who oppose us, not because of any personal injustice we have done to them, but because we are members of a corporate group which has done them some wrong or is at variance with them in their convictions. Personal enemies are those who are angry with us for what we are, what we believe or actions we take.

We may find it not too difficult to respond in love to "inherited" enemies, especially if we actually see they are being mistreated. But the test will come when some of our own people who do not agree with the actions we are taking strike back at us. The decision we face then is whether we will continue to respond as Christians even if it costs us something.

We do not need a crusading spirit or natural courage to follow our convictions when to do so costs us something, but we do need a will determined to be loyal to Christ. And loyalty to Christ is shown by our obedience to his commands, in this case, to love our enemies (desire the best for them), show mercy and pray. With God's help we can do this even when we are shaking with fear.

To forgive and to love personal enemies is difficult, so difficult, in fact, that we need God's enabling to do so. But as we pray for those who have wronged us, asking God to forgive them and bless them, we will find a miracle within us taking place. God's spirit of forgiveness will be released in us too, and God will wash all bitterness from our hearts.

Corrie ten Boom tells how God enabled her to forgive.

During World War II in her homeland, Holland, she gave refuge and help to hundreds of fleeing Jews. Finally Corrie and her family were arrested and put in concentration camps. Four of her family died, including a sister who was especially close to her.

Sometime ago when Corrie was speaking at a meeting in Germany a man came up to her at the close of the meeting and said, "Do you recognize me?" With horror Corrie ten Boom recognized him as one of the most cruel guards they had had.

"I have become a Christian," the man said. "I want to ask you to forgive me."

Corrie said immediately her dead sister flashed before her, and bitterness welled up within. Quickly she cried out, "Help, Lord!" and found herself extending her hand and saying, "I forgive you!"

But an even greater test lay ahead when Christian friends whom she had trusted turned against her and did her wrong. She struggled and struggled to forgive, and at last had to cast herself wholly on God. By faith she accepted God's power to forgive them and made declaration of her step. But that night at 2 A.M. she awakened with the thought, "To think they could have done that to me!" Quickly, she returned to her old position: "Lord, I've forgiven them." The day passed fine, but again at 2 A.M. she awakened with "After all I did for them!" Again she refused to dwell on that thought but affirmed that she had forgiven them. When it happened the third night, she was, as she expressed it, "disgusted."

She shared her problem with an old pastor.

"Corrie," he said, "you know how here in our country on Sunday mornings the church bell rings, ding, dong, ding dong?"

Corrie nodded.

"Well, after the bell ringer has stopped ringing, there is always a faint ding . . . dong . . . ding . . . dong that follows. Now those ding dongs are not intentional. So forget about the little 'ding dongs.' They will cease."

C. S. Lewis expressed it thus: "Do not waste time bothering whether you 'love' someone; act as if you did. When you are behaving as if you loved someone, you will presently come to love him."

The melody that the loved one played upon the piano of your life will never be played quite that way again, but we must not close the keyboard and allow the instrument to gather dust. We must seek out other artists of the spirit, new friends who gradually will help us find the road to life again, who will walk that road with us.

—JOSHUA LIEBMAN

When Your Mate Dies

It was four o'clock, September 19, 1966, a sunny, warm afternoon in Lanesboro, Minnesota. As Florence Eastwold Sande, trim, pretty, brunette housewife sat peeling apples preparatory for freezing she had no premonition of the tragedy that was soon to engulf her.

It had been a hectic day, the first day of filling the silo with chopped corn. And peeling and cutting away at bruised, wormy apples hour after hour surely could be monotonous. Florence's sleepy yawn was interrupted midway by the kitchen door's being flung open. Ole Boyum rushed in. "Call the doctor! Call the fire department! Call the ambulance!" His words tumbled out almost incoherently. For a second Florence thought he was joking. But then she saw the desperate look on her Uncle Ole's face.

"It's Arlen," he stammered. "He's under the wagon."

Florence headed for the phone. A tow truck is what

they need, she thought numbly. As she dialed the number of the garage, she agonized over how long it took the dial wheel to return to its place after each number was dialed.

Then she rang for the ambulance and finally the doctor. As she heard their doctor's familiar voice, her own began to tremble and suddenly she felt weak. She explained where they lived, and again she marveled at how long it took to articulate each word. It was as if each word hung motionless and suspended in space before she heard the next word vocalized through her lips.

Uncle Ole accompanied the tow truck to the field. Florence waited for the ambulance and doctor. As they drove to the accident scene, she met a neighbor. His eyes averted hers, and Florence knew that her husband was dead. Dead. Crushed when the corn wagon, the tire of which he was changing, tipped over on him.

"I should be getting hysterical or crying," Florence thought, "but I don't feel a thing." Then seeing the immense pity in the eyes of her neighbors because she was left alone with three small children, she bit her lips to keep back the tears.

But can't they understand, she thought. God has promised that all things will work for good for those who love him. Don't they know this? She rubbed her forehead with her hand and wondered, How can I get them to understand this?

The verse was with her continuously even that night when reality suddenly faced her in the form of 35 cows that needed to be milked There was help: Arlen's aged father, the neighbors. But they needed directions.

"Oh, God," Florence prayed in her heart, "forgive me for the times when I used to rebel and feel resentful that I had to help in the barn. Father, now I see that even those unreliable hired men were part of your plan. For how else would I know now how to care for the cattle?"

And as Florence got out the DHIA records to check how much to feed each cow, she recalled the strange experience she had had just a short while previous. Remembering the 35 cows by name always had been impossible for her. But one day, standing in the barn, she had looked at the cows with eyes that suddenly recognized each one individually How strange! she had thought at the time. Now she understood.

In the days that followed Florence picked out of the mailbox the usual bills and notices from insurance companies and banks. "Father," she communed again, "how good that Arlen had asked me to take care of the books! At least this is no strange, bewildering new world for me."

Then there were the funeral arrangements. This too was familiar ground. For six years earlier Arlen and she had buried their first child. Through her tears Florence thanked God again for preparing the way for her.

God had led her to prepare the children too. Every evening she had told them Bible stories and taught them to pray. The second night after the accident through misty eyes, Florence saw three-year-old Kay's face light up with a radiant smile as she prayed, "Thank you that Daddy died so he could go to heaven."

Those first days were a blur of cows and kind neighbors and tombstone salesmen and insurance salesmen.

Arlen's mother and father and Florence's own mother were strong pillars on which to lean. But the greatest support of all came from the verse that wouldn't leave her: "We know that all things work together for good to those who love God."

I must tell people this is true, she kept saying to herself. Finally she won reluctant permission from her pastor to speak a few words at the Sunday morning worship service. Somehow she felt better after she had been able to affirm publicly that God would work all things together for good.

Even the problem of how and where to continue her life —usually the biggest problem a widow faces—seemed to have been pre-planned. How else could Florence explain the great longing that had come into her soul some months earlier, causing her to arise early that she might seek her Lord in the pages of the written word? Oh, God, she had prayed, some day, some time in my life, please make it possible for me to study your Word in a Bible school. And she had been assured that it would be so. She had thought it would be in the far distant future after the children were grown, but suddenly it seemed to be here—now.

Or almost now. But first there was business to care for. The sale of the cows, for example.

And then the drain pit for the automatic washer caved in. Florence groaned. With three small children and one still in diapers, she really needed that washing machine. Should she hire someone to dig the drain out? What would that cost? Her eyes lit on the closets in the upstairs hallway and bedroom. Her face brightened. She smiled a small, determined little smile. "If I could build those closets," she thought, "I can dig a drain out too."

As she shoveled away, she relived the days of the closet building. Arlen had been so wonderful about keeping things in good repair. Together they had remodelled the living room. But then the tempo of the farm work picked up, and there was no time to build the closets Florence wanted so badly.

"Do it yourself," Arlen's eyes were full of mischievous twinkle and laughter. Her response was to arrive home with the pickup loaded with lumber and supplies.

So she had built the closets. To prepare her for digging out the drain, Florence thought, as she hoisted out another shovelful of dirt. It took Florence a couple of weeks to dig out a section fifteen feet long and from three to five feet deep before she found the trouble spot. But she had conquered one of a widow's most vulnerable spots, self-pity, and learned to say, I can do it. With God, of course.

The day of the auction Florence was almost dropping with exhaustion. At eleven the night before, the best cow in the herd had had her calf and could not get up. Florence's father-in-law knew that if the cow did not get up immediately, she would be paralyzed. They struggled and struggled to get the cow on her feet, and finally, with the help of the veterinarian and medicine, succeeded. Florence had tumbled into bed around 12:30 A.M. only to drag herself out again at 3:30 to begin milking the herd in order to be ready for the auction. Half an hour before the sale began a stray calf for whom they had hunted in the woods in vain wandered up to the barn—just in time to be sold.

My verse still holds good, God makes all things work together for good, Florence thought wearily but gratefully that night. And she went to her freezer to get out some bread for breakfast.

She stood, freezer door opened, looking in at an empty freezer. "Did you ever?" she marvelled. "I hadn't planned it this way. But the neighbors' baked goods lasted as long as I had the cows. Now there'll be time to bake and sleep and make some decisions." And she shut the freezer door and went to bed.

Where should she go to Bible school? A dormitory situation was out for her with her small children.

"There's the California Lutheran Bible School in Los Angeles," her pastor, James W. Asp, suggested. "It's different in that the students go to school in the mornings, work in the afternoons and live in apartments."

"Los Angeles?" Florence ran for a map. Heads huddled over it. Florence's finger trembled as she pinpointed two places on the map: Pasadena and Los Angeles.

"Why look," she exclaimed in wonder, "they're close to each other."

Puzzled, her pastor queried: "Yes, but what does that mean to you?"

"Everything." Florence's voice was full of awe. "You see a while ago I received a letter from a friend of mine, Nancy Pomroy in Pasadena, volunteering her services as baby-sitter. Now I discover Pasadena and Los Angeles are side by side!"

So Florence Sande and her three small children flew into Los Angeles February 21st, 1967, at 7 P.M. Early on February 25th they found a fully furnished two-bedroom house three blocks from the Pomroy's. Florence bought a Volkswagon squareback and a week later began attending classes at CLBS in downtown Los Angeles. Two years later she graduated. The verse she chose as her special verse was Job 23:13, 14: "But he is unchangeable and who can turn him? What he desires, that he does. For he will complete what he appoints for me, and many such things are in his mind."

She moved back to Minnesota and worked as co-director of nursing in a nursing home for two years. "At first," Florence says, "I felt satisfied and contented with the routine of work and duties of mother and father. In 1971 my three children were six, eight and ten years of age. All three children began to show the need of closer supervision than they were getting with the baby sitters I hired. I worried especially about Denis not having enough male companionship. All three children expressed an earnest desire for a father and prayed that the Lord would provide one. I decided that if it was that important to them that I should pray for a husband also.

"In August, 1971, we spent a five-day vacation at a family Bible camp. At the camp was a man so tall (six feet five inches) that I couldn't help noticing him. I also noticed that he never sat next to any woman, and in conversation it came out that Alvin Lindstrom was a bachelor."

Florence's three children made the happy discovery that Alvin also was very fond of children. Friends of Alvin's and a pastor who observed the developing friendships quietly began to pray. Thousands of miles away a missionary whom Florence was helping to support also was praying that Florence would find a helpmeet. Less than three months later Alvin wrote in a letter to Florence that he wanted to change his theme verse from James 1:27 ("Religion that is pure and undefiled before God and the Father is this: to visit orphans and widows in their affliction") to Proverbs 18:22: ("He who finds a wife finds a good thing").

"Both of us knew," Florence declares, "that the Lord had planned this for us. From our first meeting we felt as though we knew and understood each other."

And for Florence's children there is no greater evidence as to how wonderfully God cares for his children than their new kind, gentle, fun-loving Daddy.

What to Do When Your Mate Dies

The best way we can prepare for testings, troubles, and bereavements that come to us in life is by living every day in a right relationship to God. This requires constant, conscious working-at. Because she was walking in fellowship with God, Florence's first reaction when her husband died was one of trust: God will make even this work out for good.

Often God speaks to us in whispers about impending disasters. As much as this frightens us, we need to recognize it as our Father's very tender, loving conditioning for what is coming. He may even start to guide us along new, unexpected courses before the disaster strikes. To follow his leading when we cannot understand why he is leading us the way he is, calls for faith. If we dare to launch out, afterwards we will understand and marvel. Florence later understood how in many ways God had prepared her.

The overwhelming loneliness of soul that comes when

we are estranged from someone very dear and close to us can best be met by God himself. Time spent in communion with God and soaking up his Word is immensely healing. Not every widow can go to Bible school, but every widow can turn to the Bible and prayer.

Often directions for the future do not come at once. In fact, usually it is best not to make any hurried changes. Time lends perspective. At the same time the widow needs courage to break out of her mold and face life as an individual. She needs to recognize her own interests, abilities, and strengths and actively seek companionship. If she does, she will find it. And through every aspect of widowhood the Christian woman may be assured that God will daily bear her up.

No man is ever more than four steps from God — conviction, repentance, consecration, and faith.

—ROY L. SMITH

When You Can't Get Along with Someone

I was discouraged—thoroughly discouraged, frustrated, and disillusioned! I always had prided myself on being able to get along with people. Now I was making the horrible discovery that I could *not* get along with others —especially with one particular person.

When I assumed a position as secretary in a large urban church, the minister suggested that perhaps I would like to share an apartment with the parish visitor, whom I will call Linda.

The arrangements were made. The parish visitor was a woman ten years my senior, a very lovely person, friendly and gracious. But for some reason or other, things she did began to irritate me like a hangnail.

Linda liked to stay up late; I liked to get up early. I couldn't get up early if I got to bed late. Furthermore, when she stayed up late, she liked to spend a couple of hours reading in bed. We shared the bedroom. Try as

I may, I could not ignore her reading light. So even if I retired at a reasonable time, I could not get to sleep.

Though Linda was neat in every other way, she had the habit of leaving her shoes and slippers lying around. It irritated me no end when I stumbled over them. At last my irritation became so great that when I tripped over one of them, I savagely kicked it and sent it flying across the room.

When I was working, Linda often used the phone in my office. Conversations were quite lengthy as people discussed their problems with her. If I continued my typing, she couldn't hear her conversationalist on the phone. So there I sat; helpless, idle, work stacking up, while I waited for her to get off the phone and on with her visitation.

I was a bit overweight at the time, and Linda never let me forget it. Every time we sat down to a meal, she would faithfully total up my calories.

Our relationship got worse and worse until even my work efficiency was affected. I began having trouble sleeping at night. I became thoroughly shook up by the ugly picture of myself which I was seeing more and more clearly—a Christian worker not being able to get along with another Christian! I became so disillusioned that I could no longer bring myself to attend staff prayer meetings. I felt I already was hypocrite enough. Why add to my hypocrisy by praying piously in front of others?

This was the state of affairs on one particular Thursday morning as I sat at my desk. I had awakened early and had been unable to get back to sleep. So I arose, showered, dressed, and walked to the church. At least I could be alone, completely alone, before the phone began to ring. Maybe in the quietness of my office I would be able to sort out my thoughts.

I rested my head on my arms on my desk, and almost unconsciously began to pray. It was a very free kind of praying. I just began to talk things out with God.

"I'm miserable," I confided. "Utterly miserable! I hate myself! And how you must hate me! To think that I am tripped up on a little thing like this!"

Minutes passed. I was mute.

"Lord, I've tried and it just won't work. I'm all worn out."

Silence again.

Then, "But I feel so bad about it, Father. I know this isn't the way you want things to be."

Pause. More thought.

"Father, I give up. I'm sorry, but I just can't love her."

Though I hurt all over, even tears wouldn't flow to help relieve my tension. I felt cold and empty and numb inside. What in the world had I done? Where was God anyway? Had he left me completely? Was this why I felt like I did?

"Father, I don't know what else to do but turn the whole miserable mess over to you. Will you take it? Can you forgive me?"

Pause. I knew he could. I knew he would. I didn't feel forgiven. But feel it or not, I would act as though I was. Because I knew he had said in I John 1:9 that he would always forgive if we came to him.

"Father, I want you to take over completely. I want you to move right into my heart and being. I want you to love this person through me. I can't. But I believe that you do. And I ask you to do it through me."

Linda didn't show up in the office all morning. When I walked home at noon to join her for lunch, I prayed all the way, "Lord, take over now. Love her through me. You do it. You do it."

When I saw her, I was amazed to discover the old feelings of resentment didn't flare up.

"Wonderful, Father," I exulted. "Wonderful! But you keep things under control. I'm weak. You must love her through me."

I had to maintain this minute-by-minute dependence on God whenever I was with her. By the end of the week Linda said to me, "I don't know what has come over you!"

"What do you mean?" I queried.

"All of a sudden you have become so nice to me!"

I turned around quickly so she wouldn't see my grin. "Father," I whispered in my heart, "it works! It works!"

As the weeks and months passed our friendship deepened. And to this day I'm glad for the moment when I turned to God and exclaimed, "I give up."

What to Do When You Can't Get along with Someone

If it is possible for you to stay away from someone who irritates you inordinately, it's just common sense to do so. But sometimes that isn't possible. Then we need help.

It helps to recognize that often the characteristics that offend us are typical of us too, though they might manifest themselves in different ways. For example, one person may be slovenly and careless in dress, another in the discipline of his thought life or his work habits. Recognizing that the irritating characteristics may be your shortcoming also will help you to be less critical and more tolerant.

You might as well make up your mind right away that you are not going to be able to change the person who is irritating you. God can. But you can't. So accept him as he is. After all, you want others to accept you for what you are, not for what they wish you would be.

Aim for a new perspective. Focus on the other person's good points. When you are able to do so honestly, express appreciation to him for commendatory actions or attitudes.

Realize that it takes a lot less energy to pick up and put away offending slippers than to get all fussed about stumbling over them. Of course you have to put them away with a sweet disposition. Doing it grumpily won't help anyone. After you have sweetly picked up the slippers for a while, you might find the other person putting them away. But even if he never does, learn to say to yourself, "It's only slippers." He could, you know, be a wife-beater or something worse.

Of course if too many irritations pile up, it's going to be difficult. When you are ready to admit you can't cope by yourself, turn to God. Someone has said God's first work in our hearts is a work of destruction. We have to realize our own helplessness. If we are proud, it might take even years for us to come to this place. Having finally acknowledged our own inadequacy, then by an act of faith trust Christ to love the other person through you. Relax. Don't worry if pleasant feelings aren't there right away. Trust. Concentrate on Jesus and his life in you. Feelings will come later.

If you occasionally fail, don't give up. Ask forgiveness and direct your thoughts Christ-ward again. He is faithful. He will not let you down. Remember it's his life in you that needs to be given opportunity to flow through you to others.

Affliction comes to all, not to make us sad, but sober; not to make us sorry, but wise; not to make us despondent, but its darkness to refresh us, as the night refreshes the day; not to impoverish, but to enrich us, as the plow enriches the field; to multiply our joy, as the seed, by planting, is multiplied a thousand-fold." —HENRY WARD BEECHER

When Your Child Confronts Death

It seemed like an answer to prayer when Pastor Zakariah Chakusaga joined the teaching staff of our school on Kilimanjaro. My pastor-husband had answered the call of the Lutheran Church in America to join the faculty of the Lutheran Bible School at Mwika, Tanzania, in 1956. Kilimanjaro had become home to our two oldest children and in an even more peculiar way to our two youngest who were born there.

Now our youngest, red-haired, five-year-old David was alone at home. His older brother and sisters had left for boarding school. David needed a friend. And the six-year-old gentle, affectionate, easy-going son of Pastor Chakusaga met the need perfectly.

David and Ephraim set out to enjoy life together, exploring the woods and valley around our homes.

When they fell into the new cesspit being dug for the girls' dormitory, I rescued them with a ladder. Later I heard them reliving the incident as they sat blissfully secluded in their favorite rendezvous. The old guava tree in our back yard had a trunk that slanted gently up, inviting children to climb it. Two-thirds of the way up was a comfortable fork on which to perch. Leaves enclosed them on all sides. The faint perfume of the guavas was pleasant. Sometimes the wind rocked them gently. Up there, away from earth, it was easier to talk about things that seemed silly to discuss on earth.

"Boy! We almost got caught in that cave today, didn't we?"

"Awful close."

"If that sea cap'n hadn't come with his ship and come close to shore and put down his ladder and let us up, I wonder what would've happened."

"Could've been bad."

More small boy talk and then: "Ephraim, nakupenda!" (Oh, Ephraim, I love you!)

"And don't you think I love you?"

"You do?"

"Awful much, Daudi."

"Oh, Ephraim . . . " And then their brief lapse into sentimentality ended abruptly with, "Bet I can spit farther than you can."

The days and weeks slipped by. They were golden, happy days for the boys when life was carefree and full of adventure and fun.

Christmas came. David waited for Ephraim to return from his grandfather's home at Bumbuli in the mountains. Later, on the back steps, between bites of cookies and gulps of juice, they exchanged confidences.

"Did you have a nice Christmas, Ephraim?"

"Uh-huh."

"Nicer than here, huh?"

"Huh-uh."

"No?"

"No, I'd rather be with you, Daudi."

And I saw the two of them put their arms around each other's shoulders and lay their heads together, fair cheek against dark one, golden hair mixed with tight black curls.

They enjoyed each other's closeness briefly, then dashed off to see who could circle the school compound fastest. When they came back I noticed that Ephraim was sweating profusely.

"Are you feeling all right, Ephraim?" I inquired.

"Sure, fine!" he assured me.

But the next day he was down with measles.

Guests arrived at our house, a whole family. Caught in the eddy of extra work and visiting, I forgot Ephraim and his measles. So it came as a shock when we learned he was in the hospital.

Dave was heartbroken.

"I could kill myself!" he moaned. "I didn't even know." And with his favorite toy Land Rover in hand, he trotted off to Ephraim's dad. "You'll give it to Ephraim when you go to the hospital, woncha?" His blue eyes were serious with concern.

Ephraim's dad didn't return from hospital that night, but his mother did. She came with the request that my husband come in the car and bring Ephraim home. I was puzzled.

"Is he so much better?" I asked.

Her answer was straightforward. "Ephraim's dead," she announced. "He choked to death coughing."

Much later that evening in bed I stormed away to my husband.

"Why couldn't they do a tracheotomy?" I demanded.

My husband sighed deeply. He spoke as though to a backward child.

"A tracheotomy requires 24-hour supervision by a nurse," he explained. "They just don't have that many nurses in that hospital."

"Zakariah says Ephraim died clutching David's little toy Land Rover in his hand."

"I know . . . They want to bury him at Bumbuli."

I became aware of a shadow in the doorway. Then there was a sob and a rush and David buried his wet nose in my shoulder.

The next morning around nine I heard Dave's door shut. Dave always goes to his room and shuts his door when he has been hurt.

I opened the door carefully. "Dave?"

No answer. He was lying on his back on the bed—just lying there.

"Ma! Why won't Ephraim answer me?"

Startled, dismayed, I caught my breath.

Dave was pressing the point. "I went up to his room. He was just lyin' there. His Ma had rubbed powder on his face, and it looked so funny. I wanted to rub it off, but I didn't wanta scare him, so I told him I was gonna rub it off, but he didn't say nothin'. I lifted up his eyelid like this," demonstrating, "but he wouldn't look at me either."

David paused, then asked sharply, "What's wrong, Ma? Why can't Ephraim hear me?"

Groping for an answer and praying for guidance, I moved over to sit down on the bed beside him.

"It's like this," I began, "Ephraim has moved. He doesn't live in his old tent anymore."

"Whaddaya mean?" Disgust. "Ephraim never lived in a tent. He lived in a house."

"Yes, yes," I soothed, understanding my mistake. "But the Bible says that we can think of our bodies as tents. When we die, we move out of our tents and go to live with God."

The inevitable question followed. "Where's God?"

"Oh, Dave," I cried out, "Some of these things I can't tell you for sure. All I can tell you is that Ephraim is happy now and not suffering," and I reached over to comfort him.

He pulled away from me and edged closer to the wall.

"Leave me alone," he growled.

I respected his wishes and walked out, closing the door behind me.

Only after he himself had recovered from the measles did the questions come again. Why had Ephraim died and he hadn't? Why was he in better health than Ephraim? Why couldn't Ephraim's dad get a bigger salary so he could buy better food? Why did we have more money and everything than Ephraim?

I thought long and carefully before attempting to answer. In the end I said, "There are many reasons. One you can probably understand. I suppose Ephraim's dad—and all others like him—don't have as much as we do because not enough people have loved them or cared enough to see that they get the things we get."

"Oh." It was a very small "oh." I could see that he

was turning this over in his mind, trying to understand it. And he asked no more questions.

Several months later our family made a trip to the hospital at Bumbuli. We had scarcely finished carrying in all our suitcases before Dave accosted me in the hall.

"Ma." His face was very serious. "Ma, will you take me now to where they buried Ephraim?"

"Why, yes," I stammered. "Sure . . . sure . . . we can go. Come on."

Ephraim's resting place was marked by a simple wooden cross. Dave sank down on the damp, spongy earth and draped his arms around the crossbar, resting his head against the upright bar.

"Ephraim . . . I miss you so! Your ma and pa miss you too." Pause. "They told me so." Silence. A deep sigh. "If you were here, I'd let you ride my bike."

He shifted slightly, cleared his throat and went on.

"But you know what? I got a secret to tell you. Haven't told nobody at all about it yet."

(Could it be that in his absorption he had forgotten my presence completely?)

"Course I know it won't help you." Pause. Then, eagerly, "But it might help your new little brother who's in your ma's tum-tum now. My ma says your ma won't be so sad any more once your new little brother's borned."

I could hear him digging around among the dank, rotting leaves.

"But our secret. I can't be a doctor, even if I'd like to be, cause blood and stuff makes me feel sick. But when I grow up I'm gonna do something to help—something like building big hospitals and filling them all up with nurses, lots and lots of nurses so we'll be able to do all kinds of those operations they should have done on you and couldn't." His fist was pounding the crossbar.

"I will, Ephraim, I will! Promise you, I will!"

A long silence. Then he stood up and moved away from the cross.

Quickly I moved to his side and extended my hand to him. He ignored it. Picking his way carefully among the crosses and stones, he headed for the road.

We walked down the road together, my son and I.

"Dave," I ventured, "you know that Ephraim, the real Ephraim, isn't in the grave. It's just his body there."

He shrugged impatiently. "Course I know, Ma. He's with God. But I wanted to tell Ephraim 'bout my thoughts. He seemed close to me there."

"Sure," I agreed, "I can understand that." And we walked on together.

Was it my imagination or was I having to quicken my step to keep pace with him? Had he actually grown back there by that cross, or was he only standing taller?

"Three more months before I leave for boarding school, Ma?" Even his voice sounded deeper. I nodded agreement.

"Good." His voice was firm. "Then I can get down to business."

How to Help the Bereaved Child

Don't be too quick to replace a pet that has died. This loss can help prepare a child for greater bereavements to come.

Try to be understanding. If a child seems casual and

untouched by death, don't misinterpret it as hardness or "not caring." Remember a child is a child, and experiences life in an altogether different way. Don't try to push over on him an adult experience. Don't make him feel guilty because he isn't feeling as bad as you think he should. Accept and love him as he is. On the other hand if he is hurting, say things like: "I know you loved him very much." "You miss him, don't you?" "Grandpa would be real proud of you."

Try to maintain normalcy as far as possible. Explain there will be tears but they shouldn't worry. Things will get better. Providing outings or trips or visits with friends can help them over the most difficult days.

Be realistic and truthful. If it is a father or mother who has died, explain to the children that things won't be the same again, that it will be hard. But guard against terms like "the Grim Reaper," "Ned hit the dust," or "Grandma has fallen asleep forever." Be simple, truthful, straightforward, and direct.

Answer their questions. As best you can—and God help you here!

Don't load your child with responsibilities that were never meant for young shoulders. In other words, don't say to him, "You'll have to be mother (or father) from now on."

Be alert to fears that might develop out of the experience.

What about funerals? Parents have mixed opinions on this. If you take a child to a funeral, prepare him for it so he knows what to expect.

Cherish memories. Emphasize the good points and qualities in the life of the one who has died. Recall fun times. Tell of the dreams and hopes Grandpa or Grandma had for the child. Recall times when they derived much joy from the children. Leave with them the assurance that they were dearly loved.

Accept the help and comfort the children can give *you*.

Examine your own attitude toward death. This, more than anything else, will affect your child. Reaffirming by words and attitude the Christian hope of life after death can be the greatest help we can extend to our children when they face bereavement.

> *Memories are the key, not to the past, but to the future. The events of our lives, when we let God use them, become the mysterious and perfect preparation for the work he will give us to do.*
>
> —Corrie ten Boom

When You Feel Trapped in Marriage

"Most popular young lady of Grow Township . . . Waive Phillips!"

Seventeen-year-old Waive gasped in disbelief. Then she covered her face with her hands and laughed and cried.

"How could it happen to me? Why did you choose me?" She threw out her arms as though to embrace them all. "Oh, you're all so wonderful!"

The crowd cheered. On the edge a tall, handsome older man stood, a smile of amusement on his lips but admiration in his eyes.

Her father's Indian ancestry had endowed Waive with beautiful jet black hair and luminous brown eyes that could twinkle with fun, melt into warm compassion when she witnessed suffering, or flash with indignation at injustice and wrong. Her mother's German parentage contributed the round face and the clear porcelain skin.

But it took more than beauty to win. The people themselves made the selection—children and older people whose set of values stretched beyond physical beauty.

"You don't know why we chose you?" asked young John Warcolowski, as he swung her gently from his shoulder to the ground. "Remember the day you took me home from school, and your mother gave me a pair of shoes?"

Waive flushed with embarrassment. It had happened in the winter. She had seen John walking to school with binder twine holding rubber soles made from old tires to his bare feet. It was the stained snow behind him that had made Waive decide something had to be done.

The Phillips family was one of the wealthiest in Grow Township, Wisconsin. Waive knew her father considered wealth as a trust given them by God to be used for the needy. She knew too that when her mother saw John's feet, she would bathe them and apply a healing ointment and ease on soft socks and shoes, and the snow wouldn't be stained any more when John walked.

Remembering it now, Waive smiled uncertainly, blinking her eyes fast. "It was nothing, John," she said.

"Oh?" he countered. "I suppose it was nothing that you took Mary and Anna Kazuck home from school every day for a hot meal. Or that you brought sack lunches for two other hungry children at school?"

A little rosy line was creeping up Waive's neck. "Shh," she protested, putting her slim young finger on John's lips. He grabbed it and continued talking.

"And it's not only us kids you've cared for. Haven't I heard the old people down in the general store talk about how considerate you are, of all the times you've helped them in little ways. The other day one of the old men said, 'I declare, whenever I see that young Phillips gal, it jes' makes me glad I'm alive. She's a real inspiration to us all.' "

"Oh, John, stop it!" said Waive, and then her girl friends found her in the crowd and swept her away.

That night Waive lay in her bed thinking about it all. It isn't I, she decided; it's the example Mom and Dad and my Sunday school teachers have set for me.

Take Dad. Whenever I've tiptoed down to the kitchen for a drink of water, I've always found Dad sitting at the dining room table reading his Bible. And what Dad reads about he puts into practice.

Or Mother. She's always thinking of others. The sick must be cared for. The hungry fed. The lonely cheered and loved.

The day had been exhausting. Waive drifted off to sleep. What she did not know was that a tall man on the edge of the crowd that day had looked at her and determined to win her for his own.

He was a widower 15 years Waive's senior with four children. She was flattered by the attention of this older man. And at 17 this warmhearted girl responded to attention like she responded to need. At 18 Waive Phillips became Mrs. Lyle Chamberlin.

The implications of the choice she had made did not come suddenly. Little by little, however, Waive began to feel the world was closing in upon her. Lyle, she discovered, was antagonistic to Christianity, and this antagonism soon developed to the point where he refused Waive and the children permission even to attend church. Waive was crushed.

The task of raising four children so close to her own

age often overwhelmed her. And, accustomed as she had been to having her every need amply supplied, she began now to experience want.

Her father tried to help by presenting them with a farm. They worked hard to make it a success, but the results were discouraging and meager.

Waive grew thin and was always tired. The bloom faded from her cheeks. The gay lilt disappeared from her walk, and her children did not hear her melodious voice in song any more. She gave birth to two children. Her responsibilities grew. Gradually life began to lose its meaning, and each day was just another weary treadmill of work. She felt trapped.

As though the load was not already heavy enough, her husband became ill. One morning the doctor shook his head and pronounced the dreaded word: cancer. Doggedly, steadfastly, loyally Waive cared for and nursed Lyle, and a miracle took place. The cancer disappeared. Lyle recovered.

But the toll on Waive had been great. She awoke one morning completely paralyzed. For one endlessly long year she lay in bed. First she rebelled against God for bringing this on her. Then she accused him of not caring. And finally, when she overheard her doctor telling her husband she would never walk again, she asked God to let her die.

Sometime after that, just how she does not know, she began to change her attitude. She was weary with fighting and rebelling. Somehow, dimly she knew that through it all God loved her, that he could make all things work for good—even mistakes and sins and failings. She closed her eyes and committed herself to God.

"I don't know what you're after or how you are going to work everything out," she prayed, "but I'll trust you. Do whatever you want." And instead of blaming God, Waive began to thank him.

The peace of God took possession of her again, and Waive began to recover. During the long convalescence she devoured God's Word. But when her physical recovery was complete, the strain that had been placed on her emotionally became apparent, and she broke down. The road back to health was even longer this time, but her faith grew as her health returned.

Her doctor helped her. He cornered Lyle. "That young wife of yours is like a high-spirited young filly. You've got to turn her loose and let her run free. Otherwise she'll die." Lyle was startled enough to listen and comply.

And then Waive began to see her way out. Her parents had provided her with every opportunity for developing her musical abilities. Now to her delight she discovered their three oldest boys shared her love for music.

"Let's have a family band, boys!" she enthused, and straightway set about to train and manage her little troupe. "We'll call ourselves the Westernaires," she decided, and they were an immediate success. Clubs and civic organizations clamored for them, and for several years they appeared on stage at county and state fairs and even provided the music for a stage production put out by a Kansas City production company.

Waive's newly found enthusiasm spilled over into her church work in which Lyle now grudgingly allowed her to participate. The busier she became, the more time she had to do things, it seemed. Her cheeks bloomed with color again; her eyes shone. Her fingers danced over the piano keys, and her sweet voice filled the home with song once more. And little by little Lyle began to forget some of his resentment toward God.

They moved West, to Bakersfield, California. To supplement the family income Waive had to seek employment. But still there was time for service in the church.

Waive soon won her way into the hearts of the people of Messiah Lutheran Church of Bakersfield. "We need someone like you, Waive, to visit our sick and lonely, to guide and counsel our young people. Give up your job as a retail buyer and come and work for us," they begged.

And the woman who, as a child, had never been able to ignore a call for help gladly agreed.

The crowning joy for Waive came when Lyle asked for baptism. On the day of his baptism she sat in her pew and reminisced.

How different it all could have been—for Lyle, for her, for the children. All marital problems call for a determination to make the marriage succeed, for courage and infinite patience, for humility to confess one's own wrongs, for grace to let others be sorry and repent, for forgiveness, for understanding, for faithfulness. The turning point for her came when she had come to the end of her self-efforts, when she had confessed her complete inability to cope with the situation. Trusting God to take over had made all the difference in the world. That and discovering that Christ was the source of all she needed. Patience? He had it. And he lived in her, which meant she had it too. All she had to do was draw on it. Daily. Hourly. Momentarily. So it was with all the other qualities needed to make a marriage work.

Christ's provision fit her need, and it was there as long as she had need.

She shifted in her pew and looked at the baptismal font. In one way it had been a once and for all act—just like baptism—when she had lain in her bed and surrendered her will to God. In another sense it had been but the beginning of a continuing attitude and response. An attitude of faith and trust.

Waive is alone now. Lyle passed away. The children are busily engaged in establishing their own families. The girl who became Miss Popularity because she was always busy helping others has not found it difficult to fill her days.

When the Board of American Missions of the Lutheran Church in America called her to be a lay associate, she gladly responded. Her work now takes her up and down California. She spends varying lengths of time in different congregations, giving them needed "shots in the arm." Work varies widely from visitation to survey work to counselling to occasional office work. Her favorite is working with children and young people in choirs and leagues.

"I love my work," Waive declares. "Sometimes I feel as though God planned all my previous life in order to prepare me for this. The 'trap' I thought I was in, was just his school."

What to Do When You Feel Trapped in Marriage

As in many experiences of life, we often have to be brought to really low depths before we are willing to seek help outside of ourselves. So if it looks dark to you, thank God. When it gets so dark you don't know where to turn, there's hope.

Turn yourself over to God without any known reservations. Ask him to cleanse you from bitterness and selfishness.

Resolutely leave the past with God. Don't live any longer in the land of "what could have been."

Discipline yourself to be quiet before God every day so you can be taught by him.

Expect him to open for you doors of creative opportunity.

When you think you know what God wants you to do, have courage to step out in faith and do it.

If you have been out of the main stream of life, you may lack self-confidence. Lean on God. He will enable you. Dwell on verses like Philippians 4:13, John 15:5, 2 Corinthians 12:9.

Believe that all the past experiences of life, under God, can be used to help others.

> *In the old days, Death was always one of the party. Now he sits next to me at the dinner table: I have to make friends with him.*
> —Dag Hammarskjold

When You Are Stricken with Cancer

"I have never been seriously sick in all my adult life, so when the doctor took me into his office, firmly shut the door and then said gravely, 'I'm going to give it to you straight; you have cancer,' I wasn't prepared for it by a background of experience with dread sicknesses," Paul Lindell of Minneapolis, wrote to me. "It was something of a surprise, to say the least."

Paul Lindell is General Director of the World Mission Prayer League, an inter-Lutheran missionary fellowship group with headquarters in Minneapolis. About 120 missionaries in Afghanistan, Bolivia, Ecuador, India, Kenya, Mexico, Nepal, Pakistan, and Bangladesh carry on a vigorous discipling mission as they engage in acts of mercy, care for the sick and dying, teach, and assist peoples to become better farmers, tradesmen, parents, and people. The missionaries are committed to a life of sacrifice, and receive modest allowances. They endeavor to live on a standard that is not a stumbling block to those they serve. Most of the missionaries are lay people. The work, for the past 35 years, has been supported by freewill gifts that come in answer to prayer.

Paul has been a friend of mine for years. We have kept in touch though separated by thousands of miles. His letter which I held in my hand now shook me.

"Though the doctor's diagnosis was surprising," Paul went on in his letter, "it did not in the least unnerve me. I saw instantly that God had been preparing me in two ways.

"First, I had a problem with my Old Adam, which was dragging on like the Viet Nam war: skirmishes, raids, maneuvers, but no knock-down-and-drag-out fight to clobber the enemy to death. In the doctor's office I saw in a flash that the hour had come to take my old nature to the Cross. I welcomed it. Strange how the Holy Spirit gives insight to perceive. My cancer was incidental. It simply provided the D-day for the crucifixion of the flesh, the unseen flesh which the learned doctor could not see or examine or know about, but which God and I knew about. Both God and I knew that my selfish nature must die. So this was the hour! Well, what do you know! I was awed and strangely broken and helped by the illumination in my spirit.

"Oswald Chambers says somewhere that we do not plan, program or decide the time or the place for such crucifixions. The conflict grows, waxes and wanes, until in a dark garden some place God brings us to our hour and says simply, 'This is it. Go no farther. This is the hill. There is the cross. This is the time.' And he brings on the crucifixion. We don't do it. And nobody goes home after his crucifixion when God brings us to it.

Nobody. Ever! Dag Hammarskjöld declared: 'Do not seek death. Death will find you. But seek the road which makes death a fulfillment.' This was the course set before me now. The thought wonderfully lighted each passing day. My cancer is incidental to what God my Father is doing to deepen and strengthen his way in my soul. The former is but serving the latter. And I am thankful and praise the Lord!

"At the same time, I realize, I must look my cancer in the face. I must come to terms with pain, costly treatments, physical deterioration and death. Hammarskjöld commenting on this said, 'Your body must become familiar with its death—in all its possible forms and degrees—as a self-evident, imminent and emotionally neutral step on the way towards the goal you have found worthy of your life.'

"For this too the Lord had prepared me. A year ago I received a letter from one of our workers in Bolivia. She poured out her anguish and frustration over the run of illness among our people there. Why had this all come, she asked. Why can't we receive healing and health for all? Is it lack of faith?

"I brooded over her letter for five months. Then one week last July beside a lake in Alberta, I got a borrowed typewriter and began to think and write my way into the problem of how I am to face pain and suffering, affliction and death. I don't know if my letter did Corinne much good, but it was enormously helpful to me. Thus when the doctor 'gave it to me straight' that I had cancer, I was ready for it. My thinking was sorted out. The attitudes that took shape that week by the lake have satisfied and sustained me in this first really serious encounter with incipient death. For this too I am thankful and praise God."

Six months later another letter from Paul came. He wrote: "This morning I read Bishop J. C. Ryle on Matthew 15:21-28. He commented: 'There is nothing that shows our ignorance so much as our impatience under trouble. We forget every trial is a message from God and intended to do us good, to make us think, to wean us from this world, to send us to the Bible, to drive us to our knees. Health is a good thing; but sickness is far better if it leads to God.'

"I came home from the hospital on October 31 after 46 days in bed. I had two days to prepare for the Council meeting on the 3rd. The doctors thought I should forget the meeting. But God helped me, and I carried the ball all day and evening with much heavy business. By 10 P.M. I was dished, but recovered strength overnight, and each day I have gone to the office to try to pick up a bit of my work again. I am down to 150 pounds. Cancer is still actively present in my body, but the doctors hope to contain it with drugs. So I have been in God's good care, and have rested in his peace and love every day. And I am glad and thankful."

Two years later Paul wrote. "The year has nearly evaporated. Last January the bowl of time looked so full, and I looked forward to all that seemed to be held in promise. But now I can see the bottom already, and soon the bowl will be empty. And I had hoped to do so much more! My reach far exceeds my grasp. I tend to be anxious about this, but, of course, I know by now that one cannot add even a centimeter to one's stature by such anxiety and straining.

"All in all it has been pretty full at that. I have preached in 150 different places. Office and administrative work has mounted. Our files bulge with the output. Daily correspondence thickens. The complexities of life and relationships bring in bags of problems that take hours to sort out.

"For three months I circled around in Europe and Asia with a brief dip into Africa. Then a crisis pulled me down to South America for part of the summer. Now fall conferences are taking me all around the country. After Christmas we have a month of thick office work and then in February I take off for Zaire. I keep doctoring for cancer. The bug seems to be held in check but could run loose any time again. I don't have the strength I used to have, but enough to go hard every day."

During these months of living with cancer in his body, the experience of A. B. Simpson has meant much to Paul.

A. B. Simpson was a prophet of divine healing, yet he ministered from a frail body. Often when climbing stairs he became so winded he could take only a couple of steps at a time. Then he would pause and gasp and pant until he could go on. However, in the pulpit he preached with vigor and conviction.

As the years passed Simpson talked less and less about healing and more and more about the Healer. The joy of the Lord was his strength. He worked, not with a sense of being vigorously healthy, but with an awareness of being constantly filled with the Spirit of Jesus. He was at the same time weak and failing and yet able to run and not be weary and walk and not be faint.

I asked Paul to share with me his letter to Corinne in

which he struggled with the question of sickness, pain, and death. From it I lifted the following:

There are a few basic facts about pain we should understand.

- Pain, suffering, illness, sorrow, and death are more than problems. They are mysteries. Because of this, when they come to us, they leave us shocked, numb and silent.
- It is in the nature of man to suffer. "Man is born to trouble as the sparks fly upward" (Job 5:7). Pain and suffering do not come in the same form or in the same measure to all people, but they do come to all.
- When pain and suffering come, we feel we somehow are responsible for their coming. "Who sinned," asked the disciples, "this man or his parents that he should be born blind?"
- The New Testament does not teach that God sends pain, but it is open about saying that God allows it to come. This is a mystery. "Simon, Simon, behold Satan demanded to have you, that he might sift you as wheat, but I have prayed for you that your faith might not fail" (Luke 22:32).
- There is a gap between the power and willingness of Jesus to deliver from pain, which is unlimited, and our experience of his deliverance. Why? This too is a mystery.
- Scripture openly declares that Satan and demonic powers deal in pain. Demons can stir up storms of fear, anxiety, resentment, or despair that may bring ulcers, heart attacks, headaches, and a myriad of physical troubles.
- The Bible also declares that the devil, in a way, is a servant of God. Even his worst attacks can be turned into blessing. Witness Calvary.

How did pain, suffering, and evil come into being? In the first place, health and well-being are derivatives from the first creation. Our first parents lived and walked wholly and freely in the will and purpose of God on earth. There was no evil, pain, sorrow, suffering, impairment, limitations. The basis of life was joy. This is the way it will be again at the end of the world when the same full health again will be realized in the final resurrection in the new earth.

Meanwhile, between these two eras this fulness of health has been disrupted due to sin. And the end of sin is death. The Christian knows this. "He who has surrendered himself to it," Hammarskjöld says, "knows that the Way ends on the Cross—even when it is leading him through the jubilation of Gennesaret or the triumphal entry into Jerusalem."

So when I see pain and healing in perspective, I understand:

• that when I am reasonably well, I am enjoying the good provision of God in the first and old creation of which I am a part.

• that when I get sick, I know my pains are telling me that I am mortal.

• that when the Spirit gives me foretastes of the new creation, whether by his witness of sonship, his gifts for service, his healing, or his strength for life's duties, I sing hallelujah, for I know and believe that "we shall soon be changed."

But the New Testament also teaches that amazing and astonishing transformations come with pain. Pain is the route that leads to the deepest possible knowledge and fellowship with Christ. How can pain bring blessing?

- Pain may put us in the way of cleansing. Alan Redpath, who has served as pastor in some of the largest congregations in the world, was stricken for many months with an almost fatal illness. In his pain he heard the Lord speak to him about his emptiness, his sinful flesh, his pride, his busyness with secondary things. "The Lord showed me that I was putting work before worship," he said. "I had become much more concerned about the knowledge of truth than the knowledge of God."
- Pain can illuminate our calling which is to walk in the same way in which Christ walked. And this is never more clear than at the point of pain. Hudson Taylor sat with some new missionaries in a Chinese tea shop. Each was served a bowl of tea. Suddenly Mr. Taylor struck the table with his fist, and the tea went spilling onto the table.

"In China," said Mr. Taylor, "you will receive many blows of all kinds, and then what is in you will spill out. If Christ is your life, then the life of Christ will be portrayed whenever you are struck."

- Pain is often a corrective for distorted vision. Our eyes get out of focus. Big things grow dim and hazy. Little things loom up as big. We get our blood pressure up, and we bug everyone with our fussiness. Then comes pain, and we see things in perspective again. "It is our conception of death," Hammarskjöld insists, "which decides our answers to all the questions that life puts to us."
- Pain, when we meet it at the Cross, helps us to think of others, and to hold out a redemptive hand to them, rather than to judge, criticize, and condemn them. Jesus on Calvary arranged to have his mother stay with a disciple and opened the gate of Paradise to an undeserving

thief and prayed, "Father, forgive them," for his enemies.
- When we take our pain to the Cross, we will worship differently. We become profoundly grateful. We often sing, "Now Thank We All Our God," but seldom remember it was written and sung in the midst of a destroying plague.
- When pain comes, people are moved to pray. One of the greatest collections of poems is a cry to God out of all kinds of pains and troubles.

What shall I do with pain?
1. I will accept it.
2. I will accept it as belonging rightfully to this world. It has authority to roam the earth until the last day of the world. Natural evil and pain are the visible signs of God's "no" which he pronounced upon man and creation when man alienated himself from God.

Pain is right for me too, since my body is of the dust of the earth and shares in the destiny of the old creation. Though we are the children of God and have been delivered with Christ out of this evil world, we sit in Satan's lap (1 John 5:19). The proof of this is death. Nobody escapes death. Nobody. Ever.

3. I will accept pain for Jesus' sake, as coming from the hand of God. Jesus did. He accepted the cup from his Father's hand. He allowed himself to be captured. Job did. "The Lord gave and the Lord has taken away," Job said, "blessed be the name of the Lord."

The believer is someone who has taken death into his system and turned it into a way of life. "Death is swallowed up." Pain and death are not something that happen to us, but rather they are something we do. "I die daily," said Paul. "We who live are continually being delivered up to death for Jesus' sake." "For his sake I have suffered the loss of all things . . . that I may share his sufferings, becoming like him in his death."

All of this is strange language, but it marks out a way of life to be lived.

The Christian makes a practice of daily dying to this old world. The final death of the body will then be the final loss to which all other daily deaths lead. He does most of his essential dying in advance of death.

This should not be something surprising, for we are baptized into a way of death and life. Not only were we sacramentally identified in the dying and rising of Jesus, but we were committed to a continual repetition of the pattern of the grain of wheat that falls into the ground and dies in order to bear fruit. The dying and rising of Jesus is the authentic pattern of life with God.

The cross of Jesus demonstrated how God uses pain, loss, evil, and death to bring about good. He took the fiercest attack of Satan and turned it into the instrument of salvation for the world.

Similarly God takes afflictions that come into our lives and turns them into routes of blessing. In this way God's children "fill up that which is behind of the afflictions of Christ for his body's sake."

4. After I have accepted pain, I will tackle it and remove it if at all possible. Jesus spent much of his life removing pain. So too, from the medicine cabinet in the bathroom to the more sophisticated and complex instruments and institutions that have enriched our lives, I will support and use them all I can.

But there are spiritual tools as well: the Bible, prayer

and faith, the fellowship of the family of God, the sacraments, the gifts of the Holy Spirit, the witness of believing people. These tools are hidden to those who do not look with the eye of faith. But they are powerful to bring the light, power, life and health of God to people.

So, as Hammarskjöld called out the challenge: "Forward! It is the attention given to the last steps before the summit which decides the value of all that went before."

> *Griefs of God's sending*
> *Soon have an ending;*
> *Clouds may be pouring,*
> *Wind and wave roaring;*
> *Sunshine will come when the tempest has past.*
> *Joys still increasing*
> *And peace never ceasing,*
> *Fountains that dry not*
> *And roses that rot not,*
> *Blooming in Eden, await me at last.*
>
> —PAUL GERHARDT

When Your Child Dies

It was Confirmation Sunday, October 24, 1971. Vivian Johnson, wife of Rev. George Johnson of Long Beach, California, wrote in her diary:

My son and I were driving to church where Todd would be among a group of young people who would publicly proclaim their faith in Christ. It began to rain as we drove.

"I'm sure glad to see the rain today," Todd quietly uttered.

"Why?" I asked.

"Thursday night I asked God to send rain sometime this weekend," he said.

I was surprised, as Todd's prayers were not customarily involved with weather or other forms of nature. I asked him why he had prayed for rain. "I just wanted to make sure God was there," Todd answered.

Now I understood, as it had been three days earlier on Thursday, that the doctor informed us Todd's cancer was incurable, and the only route left was to try to prolong his life through the use of chemotherapy. The day after Confirmation Sunday Todd would enter the hospital to begin treatment. Yes, Todd and the rest of us needed to be reassured that God was there!

It was the evening of Confirmation Sunday, October 24, 1971. Vivian added a footnote in her diary:
Each of the children had chosen a verse which was special to them. We hadn't known what Todd's choice was. When it came to his turn, he said clearly and firmly: "Even though I walk through the valley of the shadow of death, I will fear no evil, for thou art with me." What a great verse! What a great day!

It was December 17th. Vivian Johnson was driving home on Freeway 605 from the City of Hope Hospital. Mixed thoughts and emotions tumbled through her mind as she drove:
Freeway 605 is slippery. . . . It is wet. It is wet with tears. Traveling home each night from the hospital is a wet process. . . . My beautiful son is dying. . . . Todd just barely turned 15. It really isn't fair to die at 15. He was beginning to blossom forth like a flower and now he is being cut down . . . between the bud and full-bloom stage. . . . Some ask, "Is he saved?" Saved from what? Certainly not from cancer. It is devouring him like a ravenous animal crawling over the body of its prey. Cancer is an ugly, cruel, damnable animal. My soul sends out curses as I see the results of its work. . . . Have you watched your teen-age child die? My feelings and zest for life have been dulled. Todd was one of my

reasons for living. I have had great pride in him. Will life be fulfilling without his visible presence? But what about Todd?

His whole future has been taken away. He will not have the opportunity to see a job well done, buy his first car, hold a woman he loves, smell pine trees and ocean breezes, or even lay his parents in their graves. Both joy and sorrow on this earth are soon over for him. . . . Perhaps, as a friend suggested, he is already partly in heaven and partly on earth. Is the transition slowly being made? Is he entering a different phase— a heavenly phase—of living? Will his excellent mind and varied talents be used in this next phase? Surely the human spirit is too unique, too complete, too magnificent to stop at death. . . . The questions are many. The answers are few. One thing I know! God is with us! He is present . . . through people, through thoughts, through emotions, through Scripture, through anger, through sympathy, through love, and through the agony of death.

It was December 22, 1971. Dr. James Kallas stopped to visit Todd in the hospital. He noted:

It was a study in contrasts. The name of the hospital was the City of Hope. And yet even one glance showed there was no hope. It was clear the boy was going to die.

The little room was brilliantly and beautifully decorated. Christmas wreaths and candles were everywhere. Picture post cards, messages from friends on the wall, and on one wall there was an autographed football. The entire team of the University of Oklahoma had signed it —"To Todd, a boy with a thousand friends." And Todd was all alone.

On the table next to the bed was a baseball signed by the San Francisco Giants. But Todd would never throw it.

Fifteen is no age for death. Fifteen is an age for fun, for drive-in movies, for beach parties, for stealing a kiss, for arguing with your father, for learning to drive a car and throw a football. But everything was reversed.

On the window sill was a small plastic sign: "Smile, God loves you." Where was the evidence of God's love? Is it not the cross of Jesus Christ that tells us that the last word to be spoken is not death but resurrection?

It was the morning of Christmas Eve, December 24, 1971. Vivian writes:

George and I were driving in the rain to the City of Hope National Medical Center to sit another day with our son. When we arrived in Todd's room we whispered in his ear, "It's raining." His nurse, Shirley, opened the window so Todd could hear and smell the rain. It was evident that Todd was beginning to slip away from what we call the earthly life. His body had deteriorated so badly that he was barely recognizable. However, his spirit was very much alive. That rainy afternoon Todd quietly made his transition from this temporal world to the eternal world. Nurse Shirley wept and said, "Todd is a great birthday gift to give to the King." We were so glad to be reassured that God was there with us; the rain told us so.

It was the day of Todd's Memorial Service, Monday, December 27, 1971.

It was raining. George was driving home from completing some last minute details at the church. As he approached our neighborhood, he saw a multi-colored double rainbow magnificently arched over our home.

How good to again be reminded that God was there with his promise of hope. The memorial service that evening, and the gifts given to the Todd Johnson Memorial Fund, plus all the calls and cards have been evidence that God is with us through people.

It was the hour of Todd's burial, 11 A.M., December 28, 1971:

The burial was a private, family service. Pastor Joe led us through the rain to the burial site. It was a beautiful and simple service. Joe read to us from God's Word and then we each shared a thought about our love for Todd. We prayed together and closed by singing, "Praise God from Whom All Blessings Flow." As we concluded the service the rain stopped, and we heard the beautiful song of a meadowlark as he happily greeted the sun.

It was the New Year. Hundreds of letters and cards had poured into the Johnson home. And then this one came from John and Leonore Lowry of San Diego:

Ten years ago, today, our three-year-old son died under similar circumstances to your son's. You already have discovered, I am sure, the miracle of the available peace and even joy in seeing one so close and dear go away from you "permanently" for this lifetime. I am sure you also have known the physical relief of being carried by the prayers of so many around you when you felt completely drained of human strength. How wonderfully aware we were of the goodness and mercy of God as we walked through those days.

Our prayer was, as I'm sure yours has been, that the Lord would use the experiences we had in any way possible for our growth and blessing, as a family, and in our witness to those about us. It would be a pity to go through such a tremendous experience and waste it.

Whenever I hear the line in the wedding service regarding "patience and suffering," I remember my feelings of the great need of patience in the months following Stephen's death, because for a long time you can never lay down your burden of sorrow.

Two things come to mind as significant in those first months: First, in my great loneliness for Stephen I struggled with feelings almost of rejection toward my lively, healthy, remaining four children. A remark by an elderly woman, who many years before had stood where I was standing, made me realize that I had no guarantee on my husband and my other children, and that I had better thank God for each day they were with me. Secondly, being normally a happy person I had struggles with the natural depression I was experiencing. I wondered if ever in my life again I would be able to see a beautiful sunset or hear beautiful music without pain. I can remember finally saying to God, "All right. I am not happy and whether I am again is not of great consequence. I will leave that up to you. In whatever time I have left on this earth let me be useful."

Ten years later? I am happy. I can remember the fun times we had with Stephen with a feeling that "resembles sorrow only as the mist resembles the rain." You may find this hard to believe or understand, but I can thank God, without reservation, that we had him and that he has preceded us to our heavenly home. I look at my four young adults, who are all committed Christians with a real sense of purpose in their lives, and I wonder if Stephen was sent for his brief time in the world to help accomplish this. I am convinced that the value of a life is not in the number of years lived. I am also convinced that Stephen was not snatched away from this life prematurely but was sent for three years and taken home on schedule.

Your first year will be hard, but don't miss the blessings that are available only through an experience like this. Let your sorrow become compassion for others and stay as busy as you possibly can doing things for people who are in real need.

John and Leonore, George and Vivian and scores of other Christian parents who have lost children through death can testify that their God is big enough to give them a hope that sustains them. Peter declared: "You can now hope for a perfect inheritance beyond the reach of change and decay, reserved in heaven for you" (1 Peter 1:3-4). The apostle Paul said, "For I am certain of this: neither death nor life, no angel, no prince, nothing that exists, nothing still to come, not any power, or height or depth, nor any created thing, can ever come between us and the love of God made visible in Christ Jesus our Lord" (Romans 8:38, 39—Jerusalem Bible). Assured of this, our boat, though whipped by wind, will stay afloat.

Lord,
we ask you to come into our boats
as Jesus did.
Even if you are silent
we know
that you are there.

When You Have to Wait and Wait for an Answer

I was 15 years when I began to sense that God was calling me to be a missionary. When I shared the news with an older missionary home on furlough, his usually serious face broke into a happy smile. Placing his arm around my shoulders he counselled me, "Now pray that God will give you a husband with whom you can go."

His suggestion greatly appealed to me—naturally! It was not too hard to remember this prayer request.

After praying for a while that God would find a helpmeet for me, I began to reason that if we really believe that God will give us what we are praying for we should begin to thank him. So for another period I thanked God. Then I began to reason thus: "If God has a helpmeet for me, he must be alive now. So I shall pray for him."

And pray I did, earnestly and fervently. More than anything else I wanted a man whose heart was set to obey God. Fine and good. Everything was proceeding relatively smoothly. With the exception that no one was appearing on the scene in answer to my prayers.

Then one hot July night, sitting far out on a pier on a lake in Minnesota, under a sky where a summer storm was blowing up, I heard God's voice again. "Why is it," he seemed to be asking, "that you are conditioning your obedience?"

Startled, I realized that I was saying, "Yes, Lord, I'm willing to go to a strange land if someone goes with me." But go alone? Well, now, that was different. So a *but* had come into my life.

The Holy Spirit began to call to mind some of the *buts* of history, *buts* that had disastrous results.

"But Lot's wife behind him looked back, and she became a pillar of salt." What on earth made Lot's wife look back? Was it just an insatiable curiosity? Or was it a longing for the old life, a reluctance to leave it? Lot and his wife and two daughters had been forcibly removed from the city, because of the mercy of the Lord, we read, that they might be saved.

God's mercy had saved me, sinner that I was. Was I now going to look back, to consider a life where discipleship wouldn't be as stringent and demanding? Couldn't I be as countless other Christians? Was there anything wrong in my wanting to marry and have a home?

A loon broke the stillness of the night air with its mocking laugh. The water lapped restlessly against the poles of the pier, accentuating the deep restlessness I felt within. I drew up my knees, encircled them with my arms and rested my head on them.

David had had a *but* in his life too. David, of whom it had been said that here was a man set to do all the will of God. David had begun well and continued well for many years, surviving unbelievable dangers and triumphing in tensions. Then what had happened that day in the spring of the year when all the other kings went forth to battle, but David decided to stay home? Why did he stay home? Was he tired? Or a bit smug, decided to rest on his achievements for a while? Had obedience to God suddenly become too exacting, too constant? After all, wasn't he entitled to a little free time? Couldn't he be just as good a king staying at home as out at the battlefront? Whatever the reason, David stayed home. And as "it happened," the Bible tells us, "that late one afternoon when David arose from his couch and was walking upon the roof of the king's house, that he saw from the roof a woman bathing, and the woman was very beautiful. And David sent and inquired about the woman. And one said, 'Is not this Bathsheba, the daughter of Eliam, the wife of Uriah the Hittite?' So David sent messengers and took her."

David, in the wrong place at the wrong time saw the wrong woman which caused a wrong decision resulting in years of heartache and sorrow. David with a *but* in his life. And what a simple *but*. He just stayed home. I shivered with the chill of the night air and the realization of the awful results of David's disobedience.

Peter had a *but* in his life too. Impetuous, lovable Peter, who had fervently declared that he would never deny the Lord. And then that was exactly the very thing he did.

In the garden when Jesus was taken captive all the disciples forsook Jesus and fled. Except Peter. Inwardly torn, he could not follow the other disciples in flight, but neither could he bring himself to identify with Jesus. So he followed afar off. Mustn't let him out of my sight, he thought. Have to see what happens. I do love and care. But following Jesus at a distance made even a bigger coward out of Peter. At the showdown when a young girl—just a girl, mind you—began to tease him, he denied that he ever knew Jesus. And to prove it, he swore.

The summer night sky was briefly ripped open by a jagged finger of distant lightning, followed by an ominous roar. The leaves on the trees on shore started to stir uneasily. Was I going to be a coward like Peter, afraid to go it alone? Hot, bitter tears fell. I struggled and struggled. Finally, with sorrow, not with joy, with difficulty and not with ease, I moaned, "Lord, you know that when I told you I would follow you wherever you lead, I meant it. Even if it means following alone."

Suddenly it was as though a great load from my back had slid off and plop! disappeared under the inky black waters of the lake. With God's peace in my heart restored, I arose and walked back to my cabin just as the first big drops of rain began to pelt down. I prepared to go to India alone.

God let me go alone. For seven years I tested the sufficiency of the verse the Lord gave me: "The Lord is the portion of my inheritance and my cup" (Psalm 16:5). Christ proved to be a wonderful inheritance, and my cup ran over with joy. I do not mean to say that there were not times of loneliness and longing. But the sure knowledge that I was in God's will bound up and assuaged all the hurt.

Then on furlough I met the man God had chosen for me. We loved each other, and both of us felt sure God had brought us together. But now my grasping hands had to be loosened to let drop that which had almost become a fetish to me—my "call" to the Nepali people of India and Nepal.

I wanted to say, "Thank you, Lord, for this wonderful helpmeet, but I want him to go with me to India." God's Word said to me: "Wives, be subject to your husbands, as is fitting in the Lord" (Ephesians 5:18). Another translation expresses it this way: "Wives should regard their husbands as they regard the Lord . . . a husband is the head of the wife" (Jerusalem Bible). The same translation in Colossians 3:18 declares: "Wives, give way to your husbands, as you should in the Lord."

So. Again there were tears. Again there was a struggle. At last I mutely prayed, "God, I have waited and waited for the doors of Nepal to open. Now they are open. But if you don't want me to return to the Nepalese, then you must release me. You must lift from my heart the burden I have for them."

Again the load rolled off, and with joy my husband and I faced the unknown future together. I looked forward to establishing a home with children. But my lessons in waiting were not over.

I had been naive enough to suppose that after you got married you just proceeded to have your family, and that was that. Even when I had my first miscarriage I wasn't worried. But when our first premature son died after only a few hours of life, I began to suspect we were going to have problems getting a family. And I wanted children more than ever. Our first baby had become very real to me even before birth much to my surprise. Until I carried a child myself I never realized how close a mother feels to her unborn child, especially after he begins to stir within her. During my months of waiting I often had imagined what he would be like: his nature, temperament, abilities, disposition, and personality. With my husband gone most of the day and many evenings, the little fellow had become my constant companion. I even caught myself talking to him: "Some day—it won't be long now—you won't be able to hide from me any longer. I'll see you, and you'll see me, and we'll be friends."

And then one night, just before Easter, our little son was born, almost three months before his time, just one and one-half pounds of him, so tiny he could be cupped in my husband's strong hand.

To begin with, seeing his healthy pink color, our doctor was hopeful. But as the day waned, hope waned. By night our baby was dead. His lungs were not developed fully enough to draw in the oxygen he needed.

"Try again," counselled our doctor, and more months of waiting followed.

The death of our first baby had caught me unawares. But when it looked as though our second premature son wouldn't make it, I was prepared. I wasn't willing to relinquish him without a fight. The nurse, bringing me hourly reports, tried to prepare me. I refused to accept the facts. When my doctor came into the room, bulldoggishly I said, "I believe God can cause my child to live."

"Your child has expired," he said.

I grabbed the sheet, pulled it over my head, rolled over and buried my head in my pillow. All the lights of heaven had gone out for me.

The blow was not too evident on the exterior, but I reeled from it for years. The way back was slow and like that of one feeling his way in the dark. My prayer life changed. For a long time I couldn't pray. I was numb and dumb. A black sister has put into words how I felt those months.

Jes' blue, God, Jes blue.
Ain't prayin' exactly jes now, tear-blind, I guess,
Can't see my way through.
You know those things
I ast for so many times—
Maybe I hadn't orter repeated like the Pharisees do;
But I ain't stood in no market place;
It's jes' 'tween me and you.
And you said, 'Ast' . . .
Somehow I ain't astin' now, and I hardly know what to do.
Hope jes' sorter left, but Faith's still here—
Faith ain't gone too.
I know how 'tis—a thousand years
Is as a single day with you:
And I ain't doubtin' you,
But I ain't prayin' tonight, God.
Jes' blue.

When the numbness began to leave, my first attempt at prayer was more a laying open of myself than articulate prayer. I let down the walls. I said, "This is the way it is with me, Lord. I'm disappointed with you. I feel you let me down. I shouldn't feel that way, but I do."

Openness brought immense relief. I felt cleansed. I felt I could begin to draw close to God again, but in a new way. I was humbler. I approached God on my knees.

I didn't demand or insist. I was grateful I could come.

I knew less about the ways of God, but somehow he was becoming more dear to me. After a while I could tell him I could trust him without understanding. And then understanding began to come—answers that satisfied my heart.

"Why," I had asked God in anger when our second son died, "did you let this happen to us? To want to be parents is a good thing. You yourself planted that desire in our hearts."

When I saw my doctor at my six-week-after-birth visit, he reinforced my feelings. He threw his glove into the sink and exclaimed, "It's not fair! You and your husband would be good parents. It's denied you. And then I get girls who want to end the life they have thoughtlessly quickened within them."

We both were mad at God.

I was disillusioned regarding the way of faith too. I had reasoned that if the Gospel accounts of Jesus' healing and restoring ministry were true, it should work for me too. But it hadn't.

"I believe God can cause my child to live," I had said defiantly to my doctor.

"Your child has expired," he answered me.

So. So it didn't work. I didn't "believe enough." But how could I believe more? Or wasn't it God's will? You mean God actually wanted my child to die and me to suffer? This picture of a mean God didn't fit the concept of God my loving Father as I had come to know him. So where did I go from there?

As I was able to open myself to God and let some of the hurt evaporate in the warmth of his presence, I began to experience deep indescribable peace replacing the hurt. The peace pooled up within me, a deep reservoir from which it seeped out to my entire being. I felt bathed in peace and inwardly became quiet. Out of that quietness I was able to become more objective.

God had created everything very good. But man messed it up with sin. And disease and death and sorrow followed as a consequence of sin. Sin moved on to every member of the human race. The results of sin: disease, death and sorrow ultimately would be every man's portion. It would come to me too, not because of some specific wrong I had done, but because I was a member of the human race. It was *right* that it had come to me. When I finally made that admission, I was relieved. God, my loving heavenly Father, was the loving Father I had known him to be. He hadn't changed, and I hadn't been wrong in thinking he was loving. He was. His clearest demonstration of his love lay in the fact that he had given his Son to die to set us free ultimately from sin and disease and death and sorrow.

But because I am a member of the human race, scarred by sin, I should not be surprised when sickness or trouble attacks me now. I need not try to "believe my way out of it."

This does not mean I do not try to find a way out. Some day a way will be found to prevent premature births. A cure will be found for cancer and arthritis and creeping paralysis and the whole gamut of diseases that still defy man's wisdom. Until then, I accept and trust. Some day I shall have the answers to my questions.

Nineteen years have passed since our first son died. The other day I met a lad who had been born at the same prematurity of our first son. This lad has undergone major surgery six times to correct congenital defects resulting from premature birth. He wears thick glasses and has no peripheral vision. The trauma experienced when a child has to bear much pain has produced psychological problems. I looked at that lad through tear-blurred eyes and humbly gave thanks. For after I had learned to accept and trust—and wait—God gave us four lovely, healthy, normal children.

When You Have to Wait and Wait for an Answer

Let your faith hang on to promises and encouragements from God's Word:

"I am the Lord; those who wait for me shall not be put to shame" (Isaiah 49:23).

"Wait for the Lord; be strong, and let your heart take courage; yea, wait for the Lord!" (Psalm 27:14).

"They who wait for the Lord shall renew their strength, they shall mount up with wings like eagles, they shall run and not be weary, they shall walk and not faint" (Isaiah 40:31).

"From of old no one has heard or perceived by the ear, no eye has seen a God besides thee, who works for those who wait for him" (Isaiah 64:4).

"The Lord is good to those who wait for him, to the soul that seeks him" (Lamentations 3:25).

To the childless he gives a home and gladdens her heart with children.
—PSALM 113:9 *(Gelineau)*

When the Answer Is No

The world was passing Marion Gould by. Severe acne masked the attractiveness of her bright, pleasant face and isolated her from friends and fun. Marion watched friends date and become engaged and listened to their plans for marriage.

Never mind, Marion thought, I'll be a career woman. Both the education and medical fields appealed to her. She was a brilliant student and won a scholarship to a college in her home town. But these were depression years, and Marion's parents just didn't have the money needed for Marion to attend college.

"Never mind," Marion comforted her father, "you have given me a prize far greater than any education. You have helped me know God."

"He'll never let you down either," her father said, "only"—referring to her education—"I wish it could have been different." He thought for a while, then added, "Why don't we pray you will find work? Then you can save your money and go to college."

But it was not to be. Marion's father became ill. Cancer, the doctors said. Terminal. After two pain-filled years he died, leaving Marion with staggering medical bills to pay and an ailing mother to care for.

Marion enjoyed the work she was doing in an office, but she kept praying. "Lord, surely there must be more to life than just earning a living. Surely you must have some plan for me, something that will have purpose and meaning."

A door opened. Her pastor wished that the children of their church could worship on a level that would be more meaningful to them. Would Marion be willing to assume responsibility for a Children's Church on Sunday mornings? Yes, Marion said.

"It called for a lot of imagination and hard work," Marion admitted. "There were no set programs or lesson plans, but I saw it as a wonderful opportunity to get close to the children and to win them to Christ and lead them into fields of service for him."

Marion understood that "getting close" meant playing with the children too, so she planned picnics, Halloween parties, Christmas parties, outings. Every Sunday morning she arose early to pick up underprivileged children who had no other way of getting to church.

God touched the hearts of the children. They began to respond. The work was rewarding, but still Marion was not satisfied. "You must have something else for me to do, Lord," she prayed. "I can do more. Besides, I should be pointing the children to interests beyond themselves."

A friend suggested she investigate the work of the American Council of the Ramabai Mission in India. Marion sat down to write a letter.

At the same time, at the mission in India, two little Brahmin girls arrived. Both their parents had died. The little girls were considered witches and had been cast out. A former orphan of the Ramabai Mission found the starving, frightened children and brought them to the Mission. Sherada (Wisdom) was six, Seroj (Lotus) was four.

When Miss Patterson received Marion's letter of inquiry, she wrote asking if Marion would like to support Seroj. Thus began a mother-daughter relationship that was to continue for more than twenty years.

Marion, not only sent monthly support for Seroj, but loved her as her own. Christmas, birthdays, special days were remembered with gifts. Weekly letters were sent. In time Seroj could write English and answer Marion's letters directly. And always Marion prayed for Seroj.

She began to see her prayers answered. When Seroj was in fifth grade, she said she believed in Jesus and wanted to be baptized. When she graduated from high school, she said she wanted to train for service. Nursing was open, so she enrolled.

"At first," Seroj confesses, "I could hardly stand the smells and sights and wondered why I had ever chosen this training. Besides, the studies and work were hard, and I felt rebellious. But I loved God's Word, and I remembered I had come to prepare for the Lord's service. So taking strength from the Lord I completed the first year with success. The next year was better. The last year was exceptionally hard, and I wondered if I should give up. I would get so tired and discouraged, but then God would restore me. I do want to serve him with my whole heart."

A number of young men approached Seroj, but her heart was set on a young doctor who showed her attention and affection. But Seroj had misinterpreted his attentions. When he made it clear he was not thinking of marriage there were tears, heartache, and disappointment for Seroj.

"She was wanting to make her own choice," Marion said. "I wrote her, counselling her to seek God's will and reminding her that:

>God knows, he loves, he cares.
>Nothing this truth can dim.
>He gives the very best to those
>Who leave the choice with him."

God did have other plans. As Seroj began to pray, a Christian family in another part of India was also seeking God's guidance in regard to the right girl for their youngest son to marry. Seroj herself tells the story:

"Their son, Suresh, was far away in America, studying in a seminary. But he returned to India for a visit and was told then that his father's health was not good. His family advised him to find a Christian girl so his father would have the joy of meeting her. So the family began the search. They had a list of 37 names. Unknown to me, my name was one of the 37. Suresh's family had heard about me and knew that I was a nurse serving God here in the Mukti hospital. They were told that I loved the Lord and wanted to serve him. So Suresh and his older brother traveled to Mukti to inquire about me.

"Suresh and I met . . . and it was love at first sight! Suresh and I talked and talked, and he explained to me how he was studying in America to become a pastor. My heart leaped with joy and praise to God!

"We both agreed to spend much time in prayer to know God's will. Prayer only deepened the assurance that God meant us for each other. I marvelled at God's plans for me. I never would have dreamed that I would have the opportunity of visiting America and meeting those who have loved and prayed for me through the years. God truly showed me that if we are faithful in leaving the choice with him, he will always give us his very best."

In 1969 Seroj came to America to be united with her husband who had returned here to continue his seminary studies. After 20 years Marion met the daughter she had loved and prayed for. A year later Marion became a grandmother when a little boy was born to Seroj and Suresh Borde. And then Marion waved them off as they flew back to India. Suresh serves now as the only evangelist in Aurangabad, a city of over 100,000, a city of 24 colleges and great opportunities to work among young people.

In the meantime, during the years Seroj was in high school, Marion had told an American missionary in Korea about the work of the Ramabai Mission. He incorporated some of the procedures and policies that had worked well for the older experienced Ramabai Mission in the Compassion Orphanage which he was founding, and he was grateful to Marion for her help.

Seroj was launched in life. The Compassion Orphanage in Korea was engaged in a ministry of caring. The objective Marion had set for herself in the Children's Church was being realized; over 200 children had committed themselves to Christ. Her position as one of the secretaries to a president of a large corporation in St. Paul, Minnesota, was challenging and satisfying. Her salary was enough to share with children of nieces and nephews and to help support many, many missionaries. And still Marion was not satisfied.

So she "adopted" Yung Ae (which means Lovely Child), a homeless waif of the Korean war about whom no one knew anything and began to love and support and pray for her as she had for Seroj. Today Yung Ae is attending a trade school where she is learning to make clothing.

Retirement was drawing closer for Marion. "But surely, Lord," she prayed, "there is yet one other I can love for you." And so she accepted Saraswati, a twelve-year-old Indian girl whose mother had lived with a man in a common law marriage. When both parents died, Saraswati was left to care for her eight-year-old brother and six-year-old sister. They were starving when they were brought to the mission.

Today Marion, a poised, radiant, attractive lady, is vibrantly alive. She leaves one with the impression of a person deeply fulfilled. Marion herself says simply, "My life could have been a barren and defeated one, but what glorious joy there has been for me in experiencing the fulfillment of God's purposes. 'Oh, the depth of the riches of the wisdom and knowledge of God! How unsearchable are his judgments and his ways past finding out!' "

For the Single Person:

Realize that the Bible's statement: "It is not good for man to be alone" is basically true. To live life alone is forced, unnatural. It is also difficult. But if a compatible

Christian mate cannot be found, the situation must be accepted. When that is the case, recognize that God can make up for the difference, that in Christ you can become a "whole" or "complete" person.

Realize also that no human being can fully satisfy the deepest longings of our hearts. Even married people experience loneliness. Only God can fully satisfy us.

Be grateful that in some respects you are freer than the married person. An old rabbinical saying declares: "A young man is like a young horse neighing when he is looking for a wife. But married, he resembles a donkey, charged with heavy loads." Use your liberty, not for selfish purposes, but for service.

For to have a sense of wholeness or well-being we must learn to balance self-realization with a right relationship to the community. The temptation for the unmarried person is to feel totally like an individual, a misfit, an unwanted, for whom there is no place in society. It is easy then to adopt a life style that rotates entirely about one's self. The single person, to be whole, must develop a sense of belonging and contributing to the community.

Don't isolate yourself from families. In these days of a mobile population many families are separated from relatives. Children grow up without aunts and uncles or grandparents. The single person can become an "adopted" relative and greatly enrich the lives of others, and in doing so he too will find a second home.

Man must be arched and buttressed from within, else the temple wavers to the dust.
—MARCUS AURELIUS

When All Human Help Fails

When pretty, dark-haired Betty Andrews of Garden Grove, California, became pregnant in the spring of 1967, she didn't exactly jump up and down with joy. With Mike, 8, and Julie, 5, her husband Art and she already had what they considered the right size family for the overpopulated decades ahead. Besides Betty had decided that steering young people safely through adolescence to Christian adulthood was a big enough assignment when it involved two, let alone three or four. But here she was now—pregnant again.

However, a few months later when Betty cradled their new little daughter, Janet, in her arms, she wondered why she had ever doubted. Surely she could trust God for Janet too. Just how much she was going to be called upon to trust God for in Janet's case she never guessed.

Even the morning of May 28, 1968, when she took four-and-a-half-month-old Janet to the doctor, Betty was not worried. It seemed like a case of flu.

But the next day a temperature of 105 sent Janet into convulsions. Betty called the fire department. The men were able to bring Janet out of the convulsions. But it was only the beginning of an anxious hour spent calling a doctor, rushing to his office, then to a hospital, from there to another doctor, rushing from his office to a second hospital. There a spinal tap ominously indicated sominelle meningitis. Then Betty made another trip with her baby, this time by ambulance, with siren whining, to the Los Angeles County Hospital.

Although concerned, Art and Betty were hopeful that they had caught the case early enough for antibiotics to help.

Three weeks later they rejoiced as the doctors told them Janet was cured. Relief was short-lived. Five days later a re-growth of the organism appeared.

Weeks of horror and helplessness, despair and darkness followed. Janet was completely paralyzed. By July 1st hydrocephalus developed. She was rushed to surgery. A tube was inserted so medication could be put into the brain to relieve pressure. July 13th there was surgery again. An elmira valve was inserted.

By July 30th the cell count returned to normal. By mid-August the hydrocephalus had been reduced to half. Mid-August also meant surgery again when the doctors performed a gastronomy so Janet could be fed directly to the stomach. But still the doctors couldn't get the protein count down or the sugar up.

Numb with suffering and sometimes fearing she might even lose her mind, Betty listened to the reports of 22 doctors, students, interns, and specialists: patient blind, patient paralyzed; patient cannot live; if patient lives, will be only a vegetable; brain damage irreparable; parents advised to send patient to a home; mother must be made to face reality, she will never carry her child out of the hospital.

"Those days," Betty recalled, "my heart felt like it weighed at least ten tons of stone. It took all the strength I had just to walk around."

Betty had been raised in a godly home in Pontiac, Michigan, where her father and mother, Eric and Era Berg, were members of Grace Lutheran Church. At family worship Betty had learned to pray. Now she recalled how her mother often said: God's delays aren't necessarily God's denials. Persevere in prayer.

Betty had always enjoyed reading the Bible. More than ever she turned to it now for help. As she reread the story of God's testing of Abraham in offering up his son, she noted that God had let Abraham go to the very end before he revealed his plan.

"I couldn't give up praying and believing," she explained. "It was a strange experience. Often I felt as though God was shaking me by my shoulders and saying, 'Betty, I want you to believe in me, to trust me.' So even with all the doctors saying there was no hope, I kept on believing. In cold, unfeeling faith I thanked God for hearing me, even though I *felt* he was far away, out in outer space, so far away that even if I shouted prayers, I doubted he could hear. And whenever I could, I went to the hospital, held Janet in my arms, loved her and prayed.

"Sometime in August or September I reached the place

where I didn't ask 'Why?' any more, not even in the secret recesses of my heart. Somehow I was able to relinquish Janet and give her to God."

Then it happened.

Betty was praying when the burden for Janet suddenly was lifted. She leaned back and closed her eyes. "I envisioned Janet," Betty said, "running around, a normal, healthy, happy child."

Three days later Betty received a letter from her husband's aged aunt who lives in Detroit, Michigan. "Aunt Helen has arthritis in her hands, so she writes only with great difficulty," Betty explained. "But she wrote to tell me that she was having her prayer time that morning when suddenly her burden for Janet was lifted, and she saw Janet as a two-year-old, standing in her crib."

Betty drew a long breath and went on. "My husband's mother, a Catholic, lives in Troy, Michigan. She too was praying when she also had this extraordinary experience of relief and peace and rest. She telephoned me about it."

Betty hesitated momentarily, then went on. "My father and step-mother were watching TV when they both turned to each other and said, at the same time, 'Janet is going to be all right.'

"When we compared notes," Betty's voice was full of awe, we discovered that the Holy Spirit had spoken to all of us on the same day."

"And did Janet begin to improve at once?" I asked.

"No," said Betty. "In fact, on October 16 she was pronounced cured of the meningitis. The hydrocephalus remained, though it was better. November 8 the doctors operated again and put a shunt in her brain. Then they said there was nothing more they could do. We brought Janet home November 18.

"Her back was arched, she was stiff. Her hands were clenched tight into fists and had stiffened thus with her thumbs clutched under her fingers. When we were able to pry open her fingers we found the inside of her hands was eaten away. Aside from distinguishing light from darkness, she was blind. Her eyes were no particular color, sort of grey, the corners were white, not red.

"We clung in faith to God and trusted, even when there seemed no point in trusting. Then things began to happen. Within a month of coming home she said, 'Daddy,' then 'Good Girl.' We began physical therapy immediately. By Easter, 1969, she could follow the movement of her bottle with her eyes. I hung mobiles above her crib. In August she started to sit up. Her sight improved drastically. My husband built her a crawler in April. She started to creep, learned to stand with the assistance of braces. From there she went on to walking and riding her tricycle. She still wears braces when she walks to strengthen her legs, but this will not be permanent. Vision in her left eye is impaired, so she wears glasses. She rides the bus to pre-school for handicapped children. The teachers are pleased with her progress and say she relates unusually well to other people. Our neuro doctor believes she will catch up with her age group eventually, only it will take longer, although he really can't tell for sure until she is five or six years old."

I was curious about one thing. "Betty," I suggested, "Let's return to that day when all of you experienced the Holy Spirit's lifting of the burden from you, and when he assured all of you that Janet would recover."

Betty nodded. Her eyes were brimming with tears.

"Since that day," I went on, "has it been easy to trust God for Janet? Have you felt the battle of faith was over? That you can relax and rest now?"

Betty shook her dark head, and as she did so, a tear overflowed and trickled down her cheek. "I wish I could say that," she declared ruefully, "but temptations to doubt still come. Janet still has the shunt in her brain. It can close up any time and throw us into a time of crisis. She already has had surgery on it once when they made the tube from the shunt to the heart longer. They put in a smaller tube this time, and at the last visit to the doctor he told me the shunt was filling much, much slower. This can mean the condition is improving. We can't be sure, of course, but there is hope.

"But it is easier to trust God now—I can say that. He isn't 'out there' any more. He's with me now."

She paused, then went on. "I've learned also to value and rely on the leading of the Holy Spirit. I try to be sensitive and obey him. Whenever I ignore him, I'm always sorry later. It may seem to be a small, unimportant thing he is prompting me to do, but I never know how much it will mean to the other person. Like the old spiritual goes: 'When I feel the Spirit moving in my heart I pray'—or do what he is leading me to do, to the best of my ability."

She blew her nose. "Sorry, I'm crying," she blinked. "But I'm not really ashamed of my tears. I've learned that through tears of concern God washes our eyes clean so we can see things in a different light."

"I was getting too materialistic and ego-centered," she confessed. "I wanted comfort and ease. When we visited

Janet in the hospital we saw scores of brain-damaged children who need love and care. Most of them were victims of child abuse or were suffering because their parents were on drugs. I saw children who had been beaten or thrown against walls. One had lost the use of an arm. Another three-year-old couldn't hold a rattle. What great need we have close at hand! . . . I wish I could do something to care for these little ones." She paused briefly, lost in thought.

"The experience was an opportunity for us to teach our children how to meet difficulty. They were so resentful to begin with. . . . It strengthened me too. You know," she smiled briefly, "you have to put steel through fire to make it strong. My prayer life and the time I spend studying the Bible are extremely important to me. Through this I gather strength and courage to face both the difficult and joyous times of life. I find strength to see me through the dark hours and the wisdom to appreciate more fully the beauty of the joyous times. If I don't take time in the morning to build up my resources, I have nothing to draw on during the day. My 'faith' account is far more important than my bank account. There always seems to be some way money matters can be worked out, but unless my faith account is kept up, I have nothing to fall back on when troubles and trials come."

Knowing that expenses for Janet's illness had totalled over $22,000 I thought that was quite a declaration.

"God is faithful," Betty smiled happily. "When we draw on our resources and trust him, we can face whatever comes."

What to Do When Your Child Is Seriously Ill

Explore every avenue of help that is possible. If you do so, you will not be haunted by the thought that you didn't do everything you could.

Take your hands off your child and relinquish him to our Father-God who cares infinitely more than you ever could. Trust God to care for him. This is not easy to do and may involve a struggle.

Reinforce your own spiritual resources by worship, reading of the Bible, and prayer.

When the load of anxiety becomes crushing, remember you have to bear only a moment at a time. At the end of a bad day say, "God helped me through today. He will help me through tomorrow."

Remember too that God never gives us a heavier load than we can bear. His grace will be equal to the trial.

Humbly ask God what he wants to teach you through this experience.

God Loves and Cares

We have come to the end of our little book. I want these closing words to be my personal message to you.

As I mingle with people, I sense that many of you are weary and heavily laden, often with complex problems. The burdens you bear are so heavy you cannot cope by yourself, but you don't know where to turn. You think God might help, but you are not sure. God isn't very real to you. You perhaps believe he created our vast universe, but you wonder how such a great God could care about you.

The answer is *he does*. Part of his greatness, which goes beyond our feeble human understanding, is that he does care about every single individual and what happens to him. Over and over the Bible affirms this to be true.

The Bible also gives us a picture of God we can understand. God is not just a Supreme Power or the Ultimate Good. In order that we would not have a fuzzy, nebulous idea of what he is like, he took up residence in a human body and lived life as a human being for 33 years. As one little girl said, "Jesus Christ is the best picture God ever took of himself." So if you want to know what God is like, read the accounts of the life of Jesus in the Gospels according to Matthew, Mark, Luke, and John.

It is this personal God to whom we can turn. He has invited us to come to him. "Come to me all who labor and are heavy laden, and I will give you rest. Take my yoke upon you, and learn from me; for I am gentle and lowly in heart, and you will find rest for your souls. For my yoke is easy, and my burden is light" (Matthew 11:28-30).

But how do I come, you ask. Perhaps it is because the way is so simple we miss it.

We begin by acknowledging that we have wandered away from him and made a mess of things. We have sinned. We tell God all about this, and we don't hide anything. We bring it all out in the open.

It was because of our sin that Jesus died. How Jesus' death can set me free from guilt and make me into a new person is a mystery. I can't figure out why it works as it does, but I know it does. There are lots of other things in life that I can't understand, yet I know they "work," so it doesn't bother me that I can't rationalize why Jesus' death can help me now in my predicament. The important thing is that I believe it. I say, "Thank you, Jesus, for loving me enough to die for me. Thank you for forgiving me. Create in me a new heart. I give myself to you. From today on I belong to you. You take charge." And a miracle happens. It will happen to you too.

This is the first and most important step you must take. After you've taken that step you can let God tackle your problems, one by one. You may need the help of others: doctors, counselors, pastors, friends, because God works through other people too. And some of your problems may take a while to work out, but when you are at peace and rest within, you will find you can be patient and wait too.

Now some of you perhaps are already living in a right relationship with God, but your present problem seems overwhelming. For you I pray that this book will bring encouragement and hope. As you have found God to be faithful in the past, so may you find him faithful in your present difficult situation. Our God is big enough, there's no question about that. It's we who limit him. We need to be quiet before him, to be renewed and strengthened in our faith through meditation on his Word and prayer.

It is our prayer that through the pages of this book you have met God and been helped. God loves you and cares.

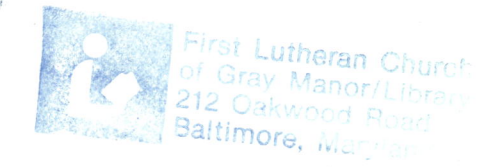

DE GAB
CDEFGABC